when life gets hard, remember

YOU ARE LOVED

OTHER BOOKS AND AUDIOBOOKS
BY KATHRYN JENKINS GORDON:

J. Golden Kimball: The Remarkable Man Behind the Colorful Stories

In-Laws, Outlaws, and Everyone in Between

Scripture Study Made Simple: Doctrine and Covenants

Scripture Study Made Simple: Book of Mormon

Colorful Characters in Mormon History

Butch Cassidy and Other Mormon Outlaws

Keeping It Real: A Tribute to Everyday Moms

The Essential Book of Mormon Companion

My Redeemer Lives

A Father's Greatest Gift

The First Nativity

when life gets hard, remember

YOU ARE LOVED

KATHRYN JENKINS GORDON

Covenant Communications, Inc.

Published by Covenant Communications, Inc.
American Fork, Utah

Printed in the United States of America
First Printing: September 2017

23 22 21 20 19 18 17   10 9 8 7 6 5 4 3 2 1

ISBN-13: 978-1-52440-464-2

This book is for the army of incredible souls who have been instruments in the Lord's hands in bringing His love to me through all kinds of extremities. There are too many to name and their influence has spanned the decades, but they have cheered and encouraged and blessed my life beyond description, and I will be forever grateful.

With this book, I hope to return some of what all of them have given me.

Most of all, this book is for my Father in Heaven and my Savior, Jesus Christ; Their love never fails. Because of Them, I have been lifted and preserved and guided and shown the way to everlasting life. And with Them, I am assured I can achieve my fondest dream of someday returning home and into Their loving embrace.

TABLE OF CONTENTS

INTRODUCTION

"Think of the purest, most all-consuming love you can imagine.
Now multiply that love by an infinite amount—
that is the measure of God's love for you."
—President Dieter F. Uchtdorf[1]

LIFE IS GLORIOUS.

In that grand council in heaven, we shouted for joy at the opportunity to come to mortality—to be tried and proven and given the chance to return.

Remember?

No. Not one of us remembers. We read of that eternity-altering moment (see Job 38:7), but for us a "veil of forgetfulness" has been drawn—something for which, says President Thomas S. Monson, we should be grateful, as it allows us to "qualify for all that God has prepared for us to receive."[2]

There is no question that our opportunities here are glorious. But there is also no doubt that the journey can be filled with sorrow, heartache, and challenges so immense that we wonder if we are up to the task. In our mortal sphere, separated from that magnificent God whose great plan of salvation brought us here, we can too often feel the opposite of grateful when the struggles threaten to overwhelm.

Maybe you feel your prayers aren't being answered—or even heard. Perhaps you feel you have strayed beyond the Father's ability to forgive. Maybe you're struggling to trust that the Atonement of Jesus Christ really

[1] Dieter F. Uchtdorf, "The Love of God," *Ensign*, Nov. 2009.
2 Thomas S. Monson, "An Invitation to Exaltation," *Ensign*, May 1988.

works in *your* life. Perhaps you are awash in fear, grappling to stay on top of adversity. Maybe you have been betrayed in the deepest way by one who should have treasured you. Or maybe you're just trying to be patient, waiting for promised blessings and starting to lose faith that they will come.

In those times, it is tempting to look at the way others seem able to surmount the obstacles in their own lives. You might start to think you're just not as strong or faithful or on top of things as you should be. Please resist the temptation to compare. Whatever they are, your struggles are no small thing—and you are doing so much better than you think as you travel along a road marred by potholes and filled with stumbling blocks. As Elder Neal A. Maxwell told us, "The special spirits who have been reserved to live in this time of challenges and who overcome will one day be praised for their stamina by those who pulled handcarts."[3]

As you are tossed about by the challenges you face, you inevitably bump up against that veil of forgetfulness that keeps you from remembering your premortal existence. At those times it is easy to feel sad. Alone. Forgotten. Unloved.

Those feelings are real. But they are not reality. For one thing, you are not and never can be forgotten. As President Dieter F. Uchtdorf says,

> Sisters, wherever you are, whatever the circumstances may be, you are not forgotten. No matter how dark your days may seem, no matter how insignificant you may feel, no matter how overshadowed you think you may be, your Heavenly Father has not forgotten you. In fact, He loves you with an infinite love. Just think of it: You are known and remembered by the most majestic, powerful, and glorious Being in the universe! You are loved by the King of infinite space and everlasting time! He who created and knows the stars knows you and your name—you are the daughters of His kingdom.[4]

That alone is a miracle. Of all He has created, of all the work He is yet doing, He knows you. He knows your name; He knows your heart. Even

---

3 Neal A. Maxwell, *Notwithstanding My Weakness* (Salt Lake City: Deseret Book, 1981), 18.
4 Dieter F. Uchtdorf, "Forget Me Not," *Ensign*, Nov. 2011.

more than being known by Him, you are loved by Him with a love so fierce it is beyond your ability to comprehend.

President Uchtdorf challenges each of us: "Think of the purest, most all-consuming love you can imagine. Now multiply that love by an infinite amount—that is the measure of God's love for you. God does not look on the outward appearance. I believe that He doesn't care one bit if we live in a castle or a cottage, if we are handsome or homely, if we are famous or forgotten. Though we are incomplete, God loves us completely. Though we are imperfect, He loves us perfectly. Though we may feel lost and without compass, God's love encompasses us completely."[5]

Think of it. He loved you before the foundations of this world. Before you took your first breath, He loved you. Before and during and after every event in your life, He loves you. There is no time and no circumstance in which His love for you has ever failed—or ever could fail.

That is the gift God gives every one of us, including you. President Uchtdorf continues, "He loves every one of us, even those who are flawed, rejected, awkward, sorrowful, or broken. . . . What this means is that, regardless of our current state, there is hope for us. No matter our distress, no matter our sorrow, no matter our mistakes, our infinitely compassionate Heavenly Father desires that we draw near to Him so that He can draw near to us."[6]

What this means is that no matter what is happening in your life, no matter what struggle you face, no matter how far you think you have strayed beyond His all-encompassing love, He loves you. No matter how badly broken you feel, He loves you. Totally, completely, without reservation, He loves you.

And so does His Son. His astonishing love for you drove every act and every decision of His life. He trod the winepress for you. He threw Himself against the unyielding soil of Gethsemane and bled at every pore for you. Your name was on His lips as he hung in agony. He did it all for you because He loves you.

As He died on the cross, He loved you. When He rose again as He promised, He loved you. And He is coming back again to claim you because He loves you. Nothing you can ever do or feel can affect that love for you.

If you feel broken right now, know this: the love of God and the love of the Savior are there to heal you. They want to make you whole. There is

5 Dieter F. Uchtdorf, "The Love of God," *Ensign*, Nov. 2009.
6 Ibid.

no circumstance, no problem, no despair, and no sickness that cannot be overcome by Their love.

Starting this minute, cling to that love. Cling to the hope They bring—that mistakes can be overcome, that any problem can be solved, that every enemy (even your own very private enemies) can be conquered. Cling to the promise that Their arms are stretched out still. Call on Them. Cry out to Them. Believe in Them. And trust in Them. They beckon you and yearn to draw you in.

And together They bring good news—the good news "that *everyone's* tomb could one day be empty, that *everyone's* soul could again be pure, that *every* child of God could again return to the Father who gave them life."⁷ Every one. Including you. *Especially* you.

---

7 From a talk given by Jeffrey R. Holland at the Provo (Utah) Missionary Training Center, June 20, 2000.

YOU ARE LOVED

"Though we are incomplete, God loves us completely.
Though we are imperfect, He loves us perfectly. . . .
He loves every one of us, even those who are flawed,
rejected, awkward, sorrowful, or broken."
—President Dieter F. Uchtdorf[8]

YOU LIVE IN A BROKEN, fallen world. That's okay, because it's part of a great plan designed and put into place to give you the greatest possible chance for exaltation. That's exactly how it's supposed to be.

But it also means that you, like everyone else in this world, have days when *you* feel broken and fallen. Discouraged. Distressed. Even unloved. Tucked in amid days that seem filled to overflowing with joy are days when you feel that nothing you do matters. That all your efforts are in vain. That no matter how much love you give others, you're not loved very much at all.

Oh, but you are!

No matter what is going on around you in this fallen and broken world, despite the behavior of people around you, know you are loved with a love so complete and all-encompassing and never-ending that it is wholly beyond your mortal ability to comprehend. And that love comes from the greatest of all—the "maker of the stars" who "would rather die for you than live without you."[9]

You are loved by "a God who governs the galaxies but who, in the midst of such vastness, continues to love each of his children *perfectly,*

8 Dieter F. Uchtdorf, "The Love of God," *Ensign*, Nov. 2009.
9 Max Lucado, *Traveling Light* (Nashville, TN: Thomas Nelson Inc./HarperCollins, 2009).

individually, and *constantly.*"[10] You are loved by the greatest of all—by a God who "is utterly incomparable in what He *is,* what He *knows,* what He has *accomplished,* and what He has *experienced.* Yet, movingly, He calls us His friends."[11]

Mortality is a dicey place in which to be. You were sent by a God who has promised to watch over you, protect you, and tutor you as you experience those things meant to guide you back home. You are covered by the infinite Atonement of a Savior who has paid the price for any wrong you could ever commit. Together, your Heavenly Father and your Savior want you to "see through a glass, darkly" (1 Corinthians 13:12)—to glimpse through the veil of forgetfulness and see, even for just an instant, what a magnificent creature you are. They lift and inspire from afar and love you with every fiber of Their beings.

Yet at the same time, you are buffeted by one who wants to make you "miserable like unto himself" (2 Nephi 2:27)—one who will never inherit the glory for which you are destined. He and his legions want nothing more than to bring you down. To mire you in the quicksand of discouragement and despair. To convince you that you are unworthy of the love that so freely [the Savior] proffers you (see "I Stand All Amazed," *Hymns,* no. 193).

Such is the battle that wages in mortality.

Though the battle lines have been drawn and the war wages even now, the victor is already known. Satan may have his legions, but the God who loves you so completely has His angels—and, while mostly unseen, they surround you and buoy you up and cheer you on without ceasing. Elder Jeffrey R. Holland wrote, "On occasions, global or personal, we may feel we are distanced from God, shut out from heaven, lost, alone in dark and dreary places. . . . [E]ven then the Father of us all is watching and assisting. And always there are those angels who come and go all around us, seen and unseen, known and unknown, mortal and immortal."[12]

The goal of Satan is to destroy you. The goal of your Heavenly Father—indeed, His work and His glory—is to bring to pass your immortality and eternal life (see Moses 1:39). And there's a simple reason behind His aim: He loves you. You are His child. He wants nothing more than to bring you home again so you can dwell with Him forever. Never again to be separated.

---

10 Spencer W. Kimball, "Privileges and Responsibilities of Sisters," *Ensign,* Nov. 1978; emphasis added.
11 Neal A. Maxwell, "O, Divine Redeemer," *Ensign,* Nov. 1981.
12 Jeffrey R. Holland, "The Ministry of Angels," *Ensign,* Nov. 2008.

"God is a God of love," said Silvia H. Allred, former first counselor in the General Relief Society Presidency. "This is true because we are His children and He desires that all of us have joy and eternal happiness."[13] That is an integral part of His eternal plan of happiness. It will never change, nor will His love for us.

And in all of it, you as a woman have a special place—something you may never before have considered. Elder Jeffrey R. Holland, one of the Lord's special witnesses, taught that "in the restored light of the gospel of Jesus Christ, a woman . . . occupies a majesty all her own in the divine design of the Creator."[14] Not one, man or woman, is loved more than another, but your role and position as a partner with Divinity makes you of unique importance in His eternal plan.

So remember that when you are feeling inadequate or insufficient. As Elder Holland testified, "If you are lonely, please know you can find comfort. If you are discouraged, please know you can find hope. If you are poor in spirit, please know you can be strengthened. If you feel you are broken, please know you can be mended."[15] All of those things are possible because of the inconceivable love your Father has for you. *You.*

And remember that your Father and your Savior do not wait until you are perfect to love you. "Though we are incomplete, God loves us completely," says President Dieter F. Uchtdorf. "Though we may feel lost and without compass, God's love encompasses us completely. . . . He loves every one of us, even those who are flawed, rejected, awkward, sorrowful, or broken."[16] He loves you simply because you are *you.* And nothing will ever take that love away.

And here is perhaps the most magnificent part of that love—our Father and our Savior pour it out upon every one of us equally, without distinction for anything we can or might do of our own accord. Simply by being a child of God, one for whom the Savior spilled His precious blood, every one of us is loved fully, equally, and without reservation. Each of us is the Father's child, and He is keenly interested and fully invested in each of us. No one of us is any less, any more. No one of us can ever go beyond the pale of a love that so completely covers every soul ever created in worlds without number. Just by existing, you merit that love. It is *yours,* no matter what. Never let this unfettered truth slip even an inch from your mind: God will always love you

---

13 Silvia H. Allred, "Steadfast and Immovable," *Ensign*, Nov. 2010.
14 Jeffrey R. Holland, "To Young Women," *Ensign*, Nov. 2005.
15 Jeffrey R. Holland, "Broken Things Mend," *Ensign*, May 2006.
16 Dieter F. Uchtdorf, "The Love of God," *Ensign*, Nov. 2009.

more completely and more deeply than any person ever can, no matter who you are or what you do.

We live in a world buffeted by temporal tendencies and cares with its unending sense of competition: if she does well, that must mean *I* am less. Less brilliant. Less capable. Less worthy. And it all becomes a sad, distorted contest of comparison in which one tries to achieve what seems an equilibrium. But in our Heavenly Father's divine reckoning, there is no *less*. In His eyes, we are all of equal worth—and His uncompromising, eternal love is equal to the task.

Elder Holland explained it this way: "I testify that no one of us is less treasured or cherished of God than another. I testify that He loves each of us—insecurities, anxieties, self-image, and all. He doesn't measure our talents or our looks; He doesn't measure our professions or our possessions. He cheers on every runner, calling out that the race is against sin, not against each other."[17] His focus lasers in on the things that really matter, not the things that so easily beset us who cower uncertainly on this side of the veil.

This God of ours—this Deity who created the vast collections of galaxies and who governs them all with impeccable bearing—loves each of His children perfectly. In the midst of such incomprehensible vastness, He continues to love each of us individually. Constantly. Beyond the farthest stretch of the cosmos. And that includes you. Especially *you*. You, with all your foibles and failings and flaws—because those are not the things that concern Him most. Those things do not determine His love for you in any measure. He looks beyond those to see *you*. He looks beyond these things to see only His child. The object of His heart.

American theologian and author Frederick Buechner wrote that "it is as children that God loves us—not because we have deserved His love and not in spite of our undeserving; not because we try and not because we recognize the futility of our trying; but simply because He has chosen to love us."[18] And in that love we can be certain. When we are embroiled in difficulty and struggling just to make it to the next corner and filled with doubt about our ability to do it all, one thing we need never doubt is our Heavenly Father's love for us. Because He "doesn't promise us an easy life. But He does promise to love us and never leave us, no matter what

17 Jeffrey R. Holland, "The Other Prodigal," *Ensign*, May 2002.
18 Frederick Beuchner, *The Magnificent Defeat* (New York: HarperCollins 1966).

happens."[19] And of one thing we can be everlastingly certain: our God does not break His promises.

No matter what life brings us, that promise is always there. As Elder Neal A. Maxwell told us, once we realize we are in the loving hands of our Father and our Savior, we will recognize "that we have never really been anywhere else."[20]

The scriptures are filled with stories that illustrate the profound love the Savior has for us. One of the most poignant is the story of Lazarus, who died and was entombed while his sisters, Mary and Martha, waited for the Savior to arrive. There were many rich layers to the experience; while they had urgently sent for Jesus to heal their brother, Mary and Martha had waited in vain for Him to arrive as they kept a bedside vigil by the dying Lazarus. Little could they have known that the Christ deliberately delayed His arrival to teach a more profound lesson—to raise the dead, a foreshadowing of His own experience to come.

The events that unfolded when the Savior finally approached His friends powerfully show the level of His love. Lazarus had already laid in the tomb for four days, and friends and kinsfolk had arrived to comfort the grieving Mary and Martha. We are told that "when Jesus therefore saw [Mary] weeping, . . . he groaned in the spirit, and was troubled" (John 11:33). His love for His friends was so deep that He could not help but share in their sorrow—just as He continually and always shares in yours.

When Jesus asked where they had laid Lazarus, Mary and Martha "said unto him, Lord, come and see" (John 11:34). Sodden with grief, they led Him along the dusty path leading to the tomb, hewn out of rock.

Then we read the shortest verse in all of scripture—one that is also the most compassionate and loving: "Jesus wept" (John 11:35). Those two short words encompass the Savior's very character, the love He shows for each one of us. He cries *with us*, just as He cried for His friends.

In his masterful *Jesus the Christ*, Elder James E. Talmage wrote of this experience, "The sight of the two women so overcome by grief . . . caused Jesus to sorrow [with them] so that He groaned in spirit and was deeply troubled."[21]

---

19 J.E.B. Spredeman, *A Secret Encounter* (CA: Blessed Publishing, 2013).
20 Neal A. Maxwell, *The Neal A. Maxwell Quote Book*, ed. Corey Maxell (Salt Lake City: Deseret Book, 1997).
21 James E. Talmage, *Jesus the Christ*, 3rd edition (1916), 493.

We know, of course, that what followed was one of the Savior's most profound miracles. For though "by this time [Lazarus] stinketh: for he [had] been dead four days," Jesus "cried with a loud voice, Lazarus, come forth. And he that was dead came forth, bound hand and foot with graveclothes: and his face was bound about with a napkin. Jesus saith unto them, Loose him, and let him go" (John 11:39, 43–44).

As stunning as that miracle was, the great miracle that still attends each of us is the love that our Father and our Savior feel for us—every one of us. The band of people gathered around the tomb of Lazarus witnessed firsthand that he yet lived, but they also witnessed that the Savior who wrought one miracle continues to work another: that there is no end to the depth of compassion, empathy, and love poured out for us every time we are weighed down by the anguish, adversity, sin, and pains of this life. That love is ours, in fact, in every condition.

Sister Linda S. Reeves, former second counselor in the General Relief Society Presidency, reflected on this biblical account when she taught, "Whatever sin or weakness or pain or struggle or trial you are going through, He knows and understands those very moments. He loves you! And He will carry you through those moments, just as He did Mary and Martha. He has paid the price that He might know how to succor you. Cast your burdens upon Him. Tell your Heavenly Father how you feel. Tell Him about your pain and afflictions and then give them to Him."[22]

President Gordon B. Hinckley urged us to ever be grateful for the love of our Father and His Son. "Whenever other love fades," he said, "there will be that shining, transcendent, everlasting love of God for each of us and the love of His Son"[23]—He who loves us so dearly that He gave His life for us. The scriptural passage reminds us of that eternal truth: "Greater love hath no man than this, that a man lay down his life for his friends" (John 15:13). And in that same supernal act is demonstration of the Father's never-ending love for us: "For God so loved the world, that he gave his only begotten Son, that whosoever believeth in him should not perish, but have everlasting life" (John 3:16).

The meaning of those passages is clear. The Father's love for you—for *you*—is so profound that you are worth everything. Even the life of your Savior.

22 Linda S. Reeves, "The Lord Has Not Forgotten You," *Ensign*, Nov. 2012.
23 Gordon B. Hinckley, "Excerpts from Recent Addresses of President Gordon B. Hinckley," *Ensign*, Apr. 1996, 73.

Part and parcel of that love is the truth that They will never forget us. The prophet Isaiah wrote of the Savior, "yet will I not forget thee. Behold, I have graven thee upon the palms of my hands; thy walls are continually before me" (Isaiah 49:15–16; see also 1 Nephi 21:16). With the crucifier's nails, each of us was graven on the Savior's palms by name—each of us earning a spot that could never be erased. As Elder Holland wrote, "Considering the incomprehensible cost of the Crucifixion, Christ is not going to turn His back on us now."[24]

But what about that more obscure promise—that your "walls" are continually before Him? It means, simply, that "The Lord loves you. He knows your hopes and your disappointments. He will not forget you because your pains and your suffering are continually before Him."[25] All that you feel, all that you experience are uppermost in His mind. He never can and never will forget you. No matter what you are experiencing and regardless of what struggles you are facing, He went there before you. And He did it out of His great love for you—a love that will never change, no matter what.

And because of His great love for you, He stands ready at every moment to save you, to change you, and to renew your soul.[26] You are at the center of all He did, all He does now, and all He will ever do—*you*, the one for whom He groveled in Gethsemane. *You*, the one for whom He hung on a rough-hewn cross and for whom He came forth again after three days in a silent tomb. He did it for *you*, because of His redeeming love. *That* is what you need to remember. Always.

Never, ever forget that, as President Spencer W. Kimball said, "God is your father. He loves you. He and your mother in heaven value you beyond any measure. They gave your eternal intelligence spirit form, just as your earthly mother and father have given you a mortal body. You are unique. One of a kind, made of the eternal intelligence which gives you claim upon eternal life. Let there be no question in your mind about your value as an individual. The whole intent of the gospel plan is to provide an opportunity for each of you to reach your fullest potential, which is eternal progression and the possibility of godhood."[27]

---

24 Jeffrey R. Holland, "Come Unto Me," *Ensign*, Apr. 1998.
25 Silvia H. Allred, "Steadfast and Immovable," *Ensign*, Nov. 2010.
26 See Robert L. Millet, "What We Believe," *BYU Speeches*, Feb. 3, 1998.
27 Spencer W. Kimball, "Privileges and Responsibilities of Sisters," *Conference Report*, Oct. 1978.

Did you hear that? *The whole intent* of the Father's divine plan is to bring you home and give you all that He has. That's how much you mean to Him.

Sister Bonnie D. Parkin testified, "I know that the Lord loves the women of the Church. If I could have one thing happen for every woman in this Church, it would be that they would feel the love of the Lord in their lives daily."[28] That love, she said, "will never change—it is constant. You can rely on it. [You] can trust it."[29]

Think of the implications of that. Your Father's top priority is His children, which includes you. "If it's important to you, it's important to Him. Whatever concern you have is His concern. Whatever you have a question about, the Lord knows the answer. Whatever sadness you are feeling, He knows how you feel and will ease the pain. He knows what it's like to feel all alone. He will comfort you."[30]

So wherever you are, whatever your circumstance, know you are secure and safe and forever protected in His magnificent love. Never give up, no matter how bad things get. Never forget that He is there, just beyond the veil, wanting you to succeed, waiting for you to come home. Never forget that, because you can be sure He will never forget *you*.

As President Dieter F. Uchtdorf so testified, "Hold on a little longer— even when things look bleak. Know and remember this: the Lord loves you. He remembers you. And He will ever sustain those who 'endure in faith to the end' (D&C 20:25)."[31]

That is your legacy of love, and always will be.

28 Bonnie D. Parkin, "Feel the Love of the Lord," *Ensign*, May 2002.
29 Bonnie D. Parkin, "Eternally Encircled in His Love," *Ensign*, Nov 2006.
30 Sharon G. Larsen, "Your Celestial Guide," *Ensign*, May 2001.
31 Dieter F. Uchtdorf, "Hold On a Little Longer," *Liahona*, Jan. 2010.

"HOW LONG SHALL THY HAND BE STAYED?"

Gaining Relief from Adversity

> *"Though it may seem that you are alone, angels attend you.*
> *Though you may feel that no one can understand the depth of your despair,*
> *our Savior, Jesus Christ, understands. He suffered more than*
> *we can possibly imagine, and He did it for us; He did it for you.*
> *You are not alone."*
> —President Dieter F. Uchtdorf[32]

IF THERE IS ONE GUARANTEE you have in this life, it is adversity. You have that promise because a loving Heavenly Fathers knows that adversity is the very best way to bring you through mortality and convey you home again. You experience *adversity*—trouble, distress, anguish, even calamity—for what it gives you. For what it teaches. For its ability to deliver. For its capacity to prove you—for, according to Elder Neal A. Maxwell, "If we are serious about our discipleship, Jesus will eventually request each of us to do those very things which are most difficult for us to do."[33]

It was screenwriter Christopher Markus who so aptly wrote, "Hardship often prepares an ordinary person for an extraordinary destiny."[34]

As you suffer adversity, you're definitely not alone. Elder Jeffrey R. Holland said, "If sometimes the harder you try, the harder it gets, take heart. So it has been with the best people who ever lived."[35]

Elder Holland also wrote, "The tests in life are tailored for our own best interests, and all will face the burdens best suited to their own mortal

---

32 Dieter F. Uchtdorf, *Your Happily Ever After* (Salt Lake City: Deseret Book, 2011).

33 Neal A. Maxwell, *The Neal A. Maxwell Quote Book*, ed. Corey H. Maxwell (Salt Lake City: Deseret Book, 1997).

34 Christopher Markus, Micael Petroni, Stephen McFeely, *The Chronicles of Narnia: The Voyage of the Dawn Treader*, 2010.

35 Jeffrey R. Holland, "The Inconvenient Messiah," *Brigham Young University Speeches*, Feb. 2, 1982.

experience. In the end we will realize that God is merciful as well as just and that all the rules are fair. We can be reassured that our challenges will be the ones *we* needed, and conquering them will bring blessings we could have received in no other way."[36]

Those adversities are what forge your character and allow you to become what your benevolent Father intended you to be. Elder Orson F. Whitney wrote, "All that we suffer and all that we endure, especially when we endure it patiently, . . . purifies our hearts . . . and makes us more tender and charitable, . . . and it is through . . . toil and tribulation, that we gain the education . . . which will make us more like our Father and Mother in heaven."[37] We know above all else that these purifying trials bring us to Christ, who can heal us and make us useful in the work of salvation.

Taken from a respectable distance, that all sounds well and good. But when you are being beaten and battered by the storms of adversity—when the wind is howling and you are being threatened by ferocious waves—it can be more difficult to appreciate the purpose of it all. When you are desperately hanging on for your life, somehow the *purpose* doesn't resonate as powerfully in your heart as does your seemingly pitiful effort to simply *survive*.

You are undoubtedly well acquainted with the various kinds of "winds" that come into your life under the banner of adversity. Some are the results of your own choices. Some result from the choices of others. Some are sent by the adversary. And while it is difficult to understand without careful consideration, some are given by our Father in Heaven.

Just as there are various sources of adversity, hardships come into your life with different intensities. At one end of the spectrum is adversity that is more like a stiff breeze—annoying, but certainly not life-threatening. Sometimes adversity is more like a microburst—sudden in its onslaught and a little frightening in its intensity, but brief in its duration and impact.

At the other end of the spectrum is the trial that seems more like a hurricane—a remarkably powerful storm of devastating velocity that leaves long-term destruction in its path. You lose a parent, a child, or a grandchild to death—or, maybe even more devastating, to the spiritual death that results from serious iniquity. The family wage-earner is downsized, laid off, or fired; your access to medical care is restricted, and you may even

---

36 Jeffrey R. Holland, *Created for Greater Things* (Salt Lake City: Deseret Book, 2011).
37 Quoted in Spencer W. Kimball, *Faith Precedes the Miracle* (Salt Lake City: Bookcraft, 1972), 98.

lose your home. You or a loved one becomes trapped in addiction. You or someone you love is diagnosed with a terminal illness—or, perhaps even more difficult, with a chronic illness that will not result in a release of suffering but that permanently limits what you can do and enjoy. Your spouse dies—or, in a storm of even greater intensity, is unfaithful, is abusive, casts aside precious covenants, or abandons you through the sting of divorce.

When these kinds of adversity strike, it can feel as though you are left in ruins. You gaze at the wasteland that was once your hopes, your dreams, and the things you held most dear. You may not be unlike the Prophet Joseph, who—after being imprisoned in the squalid conditions of a jail ironically named Liberty—pleaded to the Lord with all his heart. You and I and all of us can learn volumes from the Lord's answer on that occasion: "My son, peace be unto thy soul; thine adversity and thine afflictions shall be but a small moment; And then, if thou endure it well, God shall exalt thee on high; thou shalt triumph over all thy foes" (D&C 121:7–8).

Enduring necessitates one of the first lessons of adversity: patience. Just a month shy of his twenty-first birthday, my son Daniel died during the night; we woke up to find his body on the family room couch. After a day of incredible emotional and spiritual winds, I sought solace in my room, where I held my scriptures in my lap and sent a fervent prayer heavenward, pleading with my Heavenly Father that I could make sense out of what was happening.

I was *powerfully* directed to James, chapter 1. The Joseph Smith Translation of James 1:2–3 says to "count it all joy when ye fall into many afflictions; Knowing this, that the trying of your faith worketh patience."

In the very next verse, James tells us that we must have patience in order to be "perfect and entire, wanting nothing" (James 1:4). I knew then that my Heavenly Father loved me enough to allow me to have experiences that would help me develop patience—patience that would move me closer to my goal of being perfect, even as He is.

There is a gift even in the patience itself. Elder Maxwell wrote, "Patience permits us to cling to our faith in the Lord when we are tossed about by suffering as if by surf. When the undertow grasps us, we will realize that even as we tumble we are somehow being carried forward; we are actually being helped even as we cry for help."[38]

38 Neal A. Maxwell, "Patience," *Brigham Young University Speeches*, Nov. 27, 1979.

Therein is the gift. Sometimes when you feel that the Lord is letting you down, you learn that He is actually lifting you up.

Perhaps the wind in your life is also a gift that makes you strong. The eight frustrating years that Lehi's family spent in the bleak Arabian wilderness—making their way through a desolate land inhabited by wild beasts and venomous snakes and malevolent robbers—might be seen as an almost insurmountable affliction, a relentless wind. But then it becomes obvious that those eight years of affliction prepared them to establish the new world. Similarly, Moses and the children of Israel suffered forty years' worth of winds so they would be strong enough to inherit and build the promised land.

President Dieter F. Uchtdorf validated this when he told us, "You will learn for yourself what every heroine has learned: through overcoming challenges come growth and strength. It is your reaction to adversity, not the adversity itself, that determines how your life's story will develop. . . . Adversity helps us to develop a depth of character that comes in no other way. Our loving Heavenly Father has set us in a world filled with challenges and trials so that we, through opposition, can learn wisdom, become stronger, and experience joy."[39]

Perhaps instead of asking that the winds cease, you might ask that the Lord consecrate them for your gain. During a very difficult period of my life, that's exactly what I learned I needed to do if I was to survive emotionally and spiritually.

On my forty-ninth birthday, my seventeen-year-old son committed suicide. A few months later, I learned that my husband was abusing drugs. A few months after that, we moved—and a few months after *that*, my husband left the Church and our marriage. Two months later, I was laid off from my job of thirteen years. And just a week after I found another job, I woke up to find that Daniel had died. It was a series of real hurricanes.

But I found something soul-affirming through it all. The wind that seemed to batter me so mercilessly at the suicide of my seventeen-year-old son actually gave me the strength to survive a divorce, the loss of my job, and the death of a second son within the next year. When those hurricanes slammed into me with all their terrifying force, I was able to stand firmly rooted in faith because of what the earlier winds had made of me.

I don't know what your particular adversities are, but I can imagine that you have had—or will almost certainly have—the same sort of experience.

---

39 Dieter F. Uchtdorf, *Your Happily Ever After* (Salt Lake City: Deseret Book, 2011).

One set of winds will make of you a strong fortress that will withstand whatever else comes your way.

The process of obtaining that strength can be painful in itself. C. S. Lewis created a fitting analogy of it all:

> Imagine yourself as a living house. God comes in to rebuild that house. At first, perhaps, you can understand what He is doing. He is getting the drains right and stopping the leaks in the roof and so on; you knew that those jobs needed doing and so you are not surprised. But presently He starts knocking the house about in a way that hurts abominably and does not seem to make any sense. What on earth is He up to? The explanation is that He is building quite a different house from the one you thought of—throwing out a new wing here, putting on an extra floor there, running up towers, making courtyards. You thought you were being made into a decent little cottage: but He is building a palace. He intends to come and live in it Himself.[40]

In a letter to a friend whose wife had just died, Lewis wrote, "We are not necessarily doubting that God will do the best for us; we are wondering how painful the best will turn out to be."[41] While you *can't* yet put a finger on how painful things may yet become, you *can* know one thing with absolute certainty: there may be pain and anguish and you may even be tried to your very limit, but God will make all things work for your best. And in the end, after the winds die down, you will be stronger and better able to face the next wind that comes along. You do not know what lies ahead, but the Lord does. And He knows how to most perfectly prepare you for it. As Elder Holland says, "It is the plain and very sobering truth that before great moments, certainly before great spiritual moments, there can come adversity, opposition, and darkness. Life has some of these moments for us, and occasionally they come just as we are approaching an important decision or a significant step in our lives."[42]

As you focus on the damage caused by the wind, as you stand in the rubble of what used to be your hopes and dreams, you might fail to see that

---

40 C. S. Lewis, *Mere Christianity* (London: Geoffrey Bles, 1952).
41 C. S. Lewis, *Letters of C. S. Lewis*, ed. Warnie Lewis, 1966.
42 Jeffrey R. Holland, "Cast Not Away Therefore Your Confidence," *Brigham Young University Speeches*, March 2, 1999.

the wind itself actually *delivers you*. The Jaredites, eager to reach the promised land, fashioned watertight vessels that would carry them across the water. The brother of Jared, exhibiting enormous and almost incomprehensible faith, invited the Lord to provide the light that would illuminate their vessels by touching sixteen stones with His finger (see Ether 3:1–6). After all their preparations, "they set forth into the sea, commending themselves unto the Lord their God" (Ether 6:4).

What happened next teaches a valuable lesson about the wind:

> And it came to pass that the Lord God caused that there should be a *furious wind* upon the face of the waters, towards the promised land; and thus they were *tossed upon the waves of the sea* before the wind.
>
> And it came to pass that they were many times buried in the depths of the sea, because of the mountain waves which broke upon them, and also the great and terrible tempests which were caused by the fierceness of the wind. . . .
>
> And it came to pass that *the wind never did cease to blow towards the promised land* while they were upon the waters; and thus they were driven forth before the wind. (Ether 6:5–6, 8; emphasis added)

The airtight vessels that the brother of Jared fashioned had no sails, no rudders, no engines—no way of powering or steering themselves toward their destination. It was only by the power of the wind, sometimes coming in "mountain waves which broke upon them" and "great and terrible tempests," that the boats were driven to their destination. During that journey, shut in the windowless vessels and unable to see for themselves what was happening, it is certainly easy to imagine that those intrepid passengers may have seen those winds as adversity—may have been absolutely terrified about what was happening.

Yet those winds were actually deliverance. Instead of bobbing aimlessly at sea for the rest of their lives, unable to power their own crafts, the Jaredites were driven by wind that "never did cease to blow" until they were delivered and deposited on the shores of the promised land.

Lehi and his family had a similar experience. With the Lord's blueprint, Nephi located ore and fashioned tools and built a ship—fueled not by his own experience, but tutored completely by the Lord. After his family had made all the necessary preparations, they "put forth into the sea and were driven forth before the wind towards the promised land" (1 Nephi 18:8). They, like the Jaredites, did not drift aimlessly in a vast sea. Instead, they were delivered by the winds.

During those times when the wind is blowing, *especially when it is howling with tremendous fury,* you may not realize you are being delivered. You may feel you are being battered and bruised and tossed against the crushing extremities. But as Elder Maxwell so vividly reminded us, "Even when a seeming undertow grasps us, somehow, in the tumbling, we are being carried forward."[43] Not only that, but every one of us has what Elder Holland described as a "safe harbor"— "the power of Christ."[44] If you do not recognize those safe harbors while you are being tossed and thrown about, they will still be there for you once the storm has died down. Remember this: As Nephi built the ship that would carry his family to the promised land, the Lord told him that only *after* he arrived in the promised land would he know "that I, the Lord, did deliver you" (1 Nephi 17:14). Maybe you can recognize His hand *only after the trials cease.*

As you are driven by those winds of adversity, even as they rage in all their fury, a life-altering question arises: how will you react?

Scattered across the opening pages of the Book of Mormon are examples of possible reactions. In almost every case, Laman and Lemuel murmured and turned their backs on the Lord. In almost every case, Nephi instead sought the Lord, exhibiting faith in Him and calling on Him for help.

At one point, as their ship was being driven back on the waters, Nephi gives us the pattern for a righteous response. Despite being bound and physically harmed by his brothers, he explains that "I did look unto my God, and I did praise him all the day long; and I did not murmur against the Lord because of mine afflictions" (1 Nephi 18:16).

And what of the Jaredites, they who had been buried by mountainous waves and subjected to great and terrible tempests? The *first thing* they did when they set foot on the shores of the promised land was to kneel, humble themselves before the Lord, and "shed tears of joy before the Lord, because of the multitude of his tender mercies over them" (Ether 6:12).

Mountainous waves and *great tempests* were "tender mercies"? Yes. It is those tender mercies, sometimes carried on the wind of adversity, that are

43 Neal A. Maxell, *The Neal A. Maxwell Quote Book,* ed. Corey H. Maxwell (Salt Lake City: Deseret Book, 1997).
44 Jeffrey R. Holland, "Safety for the Soul," *Ensign,* Nov. 2009.

over all those that the Lord has chosen—all those He will make "mighty even unto the power of deliverance" (1 Nephi 1:20). And that includes you.

The very experience of adversity can be the thing that makes of your life things you would never have imagined. Elder Holland pointed out, "Fighting through darkness and despair and pleading for the light is what opened this dispensation. It is what keeps it going, and it is what will keep you going."[45]

It is to the Lord we must turn in those times of darkness and despair, *especially* when the wind is at its most furious, because it is through the Lord that all things—including deliverance—are possible. As the Lord prepared Nephi to embark on his journey to the promised land, He explained that it is God who nourishes us, strengthens us, and provides the means for us as we journey throughout this wilderness we know as mortality. He told Nephi—and he tells you and all of us—that "I will be your light in the wilderness; and I will prepare the way before you, . . . ye shall be led towards the promised land; and ye shall know that it is by me that ye are led" (1 Nephi 17:13).

As Isaiah spoke of the Savior's Atonement, he prophesied, "He hath borne our grief, and carried our sorrows" (Isaiah 53:4). Latter-day scripture emphasizes that the Savior "came into the world . . . to bear the sins of the world" (D&C 76:41). An oft-sung hymn invites us to "hear [our] great Deliv'rer's voice!" ("Israel, Israel, God Is Calling," *Hymns*, no. 7). Of those passages and of the great Redeemer, Elder Holland says:

> *Bear, borne, carry, deliver.* These are powerful, heartening messianic words. They convey help and hope for safe movement from where we are to where we need to be—but cannot get without assistance. These words also connote burden, struggle, and fatigue—words most appropriate in describing the mission of Him who, at unspeakable cost, lifts us up when we have fallen, carries us forward when strength is gone, delivers us safely home when safety seems far beyond our reach. "My Father sent me," He said, "that I might be lifted up upon the cross; . . . that as I have been lifted up . . . even so should men be lifted up . . . to . . . me." (3 Nephi 27:14)[46]

---

45 Jeffrey R. Holland, *Created for Greater Things* (Salt Lake City: Deseret Book, 2011).
46 Jeffrey R. Holland, "Behold Thy Mother," *Ensign*, Nov. 2015.

The Savior has the ability to carry you forward and lighten your load and deliver you safely home because He *knows* you. Of the Savior's infinite Atonement, Alma testified, "And he shall go forth, suffering pains and afflictions and temptations of every kind; and this that the word might be fulfilled which saith he will take upon him the pains and the sicknesses of his people . . . and he will take upon him their infirmities, that his bowels may be filled with mercy, according to the flesh, that he may know according to the flesh how to succor his people according to their infirmities" (Alma 7:11–12).

Sister Linda Reeves, former second counselor in the General Relief Society Presidency, said, "Dear sisters, our Heavenly Father and our Savior, Jesus Christ, know us and love us. They know when we are in pain or suffering in any way. . . . They feel the depth of our suffering, and we can feel of Their love and compassion in our suffering."[47]

To know that the Savior suffered all things before you leads to an increased ability to weather the storm. That knowledge gives you a greater reliance on Him and a hope that could come in no other way. Elder Holland wrote of it, "Christ walked the path every mortal is called to walk so that He would know how to succor and strengthen us in our most difficult times. He knows the deepest and most personal burdens we carry. He knows the most public and poignant pains we bear. He descended below *all* such grief in order that he might lift us above it. There is no anguish or sorrow or sadness in life that He has not suffered in our behalf and borne away upon His own valiant and compassionate shoulders."[48]

As you face the adversity that will surely come, remember this counsel from Elder Holland:

> There *is* help. There *is* happiness. There really *is* light at the end of the tunnel. It is the Light of the World, the Bright and Morning Star, the "light that is endless, that can never be darkened" (see John 8:12; Rev 22:16; Mosiah 16:9). It is the very Son of God Himself. . . . To any who may be struggling to see that light and find that hope, I say: Hold on. Keep trying. God loves you. Things will improve. Christ

---

47 Linda S. Reeves, "The Lord Has Not Forgotten You," *Ensign*, Nov. 2012.
48 Jeffrey R. Holland, *Christ and the New Covenant: The Messianic Message of the Book of Mormon* (Salt Lake City: Deseret Book, 1997), 223–224; emphasis added.

comes to you in His "more excellent ministry" with a future of "better promises."[49]

You don't know the meaning of all things, nor do you know what the outcome will be; that is part of living by faith. But no matter what you're called on to experience in this life, you can know one thing for certain: your Heavenly Father and your Savior, Jesus Christ, love you and know you personally. They are keenly aware of your trials and difficulties in this life. They intimately know the winds—both those They send into your life and those that stem from a different source. Their perfect love for you is the one thing on which you can *always* rely.

When this life is over, you will see with great clarity how the Lord carried you through storms you never could have endured alone. You will also see that seemingly random or chaotic events were all part of a plan carefully designed for your growth and your blessing.

The winds *will* come. May you recognize them as winds of deliverance that will teach you patience and strengthen you and eventually bring you to your promised land. And may you recognize that while they howl, that with God—who loves you with a perfect love and who wants nothing more than to welcome you home and enfold you safely in His loving arms—nothing is impossible.

As Elder Holland so poignantly testified, "Even if you cannot always see that silver lining on your clouds, God can, for He is the very source of the light you seek. He does love you, and He knows your fears. He hears your prayers. He is your Heavenly Father, and surely He matches with His own the tears His children shed."[50]

49 Jeffrey R. Holland, "An High Priest of Good Things to Come," *Ensign*, Nov. 1999.
50 Jeffrey R. Holland, *Created for Greater Things* (Salt Lake City: Deseret Book, 2011).

"O GOD, WHERE ART THOU?"
Believing Your Prayers Will Be Answered

> *"Hold fast to what you already know and*
> *stand strong until additional knowledge comes. . . .*
> *You have more faith than you think you do."*
> —Elder Jeffrey R. Holland[51]

AT A TIME WHEN THE Saints were being viciously persecuted in Missouri, even to a point of being driven out of Jackson County, the Lord told the Prophet Joseph Smith, "fear not, let your hearts be comforted; . . . for your prayers have entered into the ears of the Lord of Sabaoth, and are recorded with this seal and testament—the Lord hath sworn and decreed that they shall be granted" (D&C 98:1–2).

It's difficult to imagine a time or a people for whom prayer must have been more pleading. And it's difficult to imagine a people who might have been more convinced that their prayers weren't being heard or answered. They were being driven from their homes, their property was being destroyed, they were being tarred and feathered, and their very lives were in danger. Some, in fact, *did* lose their lives as a consequence of their faith.

And it all kept happening despite the constant, fervent prayers of the faithful.

Their pleas must have been poignant and desperate as they flung themselves to their knees. What pain must have laced their heavenward cries. And at least a handful must have wondered when or whether those tender prayers would ever be answered.

You might be feeling the same way about your own circumstance.

The subject of your frantic petitions to God probably differs from those of the early Saints. That doesn't matter. Regardless of circumstance, your

---

51 Jeffrey R. Holland, "Lord, I Believe," *Ensign*, May 2013.

prayers may be every bit as dire and anxious as were those of the Saints who gathered their children into their skirts and pleaded for their very lives. And your heart is likely to be every bit as inconsolable and despairing if it seems your prayers are not being answered.

Look at that promise given to the Prophet-leader of those careworn Saints by the Lord Himself. He confirmed that their prayers had entered His ears. He covenanted that their prayers had been recorded with a seal and testament. And He promised that their prayers would be answered.

To those of us who have scanned the pages of history, it may not seem at first glance that those prayers *were* answered. The Saints continued to be driven out—exterminated, in some cases. The tarring and feathering continued. Homes were torched and plundered. Their Prophet was martyred. They were thrust out onto the frozen prairies, homeless and seemingly forsaken, like so much rubble. They were forced to turn their backs on a temple they had built with pure grit and determination. Shallow graves—some so small they could accommodate only an infant—dotted the landscape between Nauvoo and their new home in the Rocky Mountains.

But—and this is the important part—most of them *did* arrive in the Rocky Mountains. (And those who didn't? Remember William Clayton's stirring words: "And if we die before our journey's through, Happy day! All is well!") Many of them found peace at their journey's end, whether that consisted of arrival in the valley or arrival in the world of spirits. Could *that* have been the answer to their prayers? In the next breath of that revelation, the Lord promised, "all things wherewith you have been afflicted shall work together for your good, and to my name's glory" (D&C 98:3). It was an answer that came, but only after waiting patiently on the Lord.

Does this same thing happen in our day? Has this same thing happened to you?

It's easy to look back with the perspective of hindsight and recognize that imploring prayers were indeed answered, eventually. But when you're in the thick of it, sometimes it simply seems that no one is listening, much less answering. In such a case, it can be easy to feel forgotten. Abandoned.

An even more difficult scenario occurs when, after having sublime experiences with answered prayers, you crash-land into a time or situation in which the channels of communication with heaven seem forever silenced. You know how to pray. You've done it before. And you know how to recognize answers, because you've received them before.

Suddenly, you find yourself in strange, uncharted territory. For now, there's no map to get you safely to your destination. Guideposts have vanished. The "two-way radio" upon which you've relied is no longer reaching the heavens. Sometimes you seem to hear nothing but static; sometimes you seem to hear nothing at all.

In those times, what is happening? Does heaven ever turn a deaf ear?

No—the very thought makes reason stare.

The God to whom we pray can hear even the softest mewling of a newborn kitten, even the sound of an aspen leaf as it makes its gentle descent to Earth, carried on a quiet breeze. There is no deafness in those holy ears. Certainly He hears you, even when your prayer is whispered only in the silent chambers of your heart.

In fact, we have been assured that our prayers *are* heard. Elder Jeffrey R. Holland wrote, "Your Father in Heaven knows your name and knows your circumstance. *He hears your prayers.* He knows your hopes and dreams, including your fears and frustrations."[52]

That's a bold statement, and within it are some remarkable and unflinching notions. He hears, this God of ours. And He weighs whatever He hears from you against your hopes and dreams, your fears and frustrations. Nothing for Him is out of context. He knows your circumstance, the state of your heart and soul, even better than you yourself know it. There is nothing you can tell Him of your desperate situation that He hasn't already seen and understood.

What, then, is happening? Why does it seem your prayers are unheard—or, at the very least, go unanswered?

Perhaps the answer comes, but it is not what you expected. As you wait in anguish for heaven to respond, you may not recognize what has already been sent from a loving Father. The answer may be there, waiting to be identified, while you continue to cry for relief from a Father who has already poured out His loving response.

It's like this: Imagine you are praying for a loaf of bread. In your heart, you decide that what you need is a loaf of chewy, crusty, sourdough bread. Your prayer is fervent, your faith solid. And so you continue, step after step along your journey, looking everywhere for the sought-after loaf of sourdough bread. When days and weeks and even months go by, your faith

52 Jeffrey R. Holland, *Created for Greater Things* (Salt Lake City: Deseret Book, 2011); emphasis added.

becomes frayed around the edges as you still search in vain for the loaf of sourdough bread. Your conclusion seems all too obvious: Your prayer has not been answered.

But what if, when you prayed for that loaf of bread, your Father knew that you needed pumpernickel bread? After all, "your Father knoweth what things ye have need of, before ye ask him" (Matthew 6:8). And so, in His love for you and His desire to answer your prayer, He litters your path with rounded loaves of perfectly spiced pumpernickel bread. But you, in your desperate search for that loaf of sourdough, miss it all. His answer is evident all around you, a testament of His love and His generosity of spirit, but you are blinded, seeking instead the thing you expected—that thing you thought you needed.

Remember too that the answer may not come in exactly the way you expect. Elder Holland reminds us, "Please know that your Father in Heaven loves you and so does His Only Begotten Son. When They speak to you— and They will—it will not be in the wind, nor in the earthquake, nor in the fire, but it will be with a voice still and small, a voice tender and kind. It will be with the tongue of angels."[53]

Sometimes you may not receive an answer because there is no place for God to put it. Your Father may have the perfect answer to your determined prayer, but you have not yet created a space into which he can lovingly tuck that answer. In a devotional address at BYU–Hawaii, CES instructor S. Michael Wilcox said that "sometimes the reason the Lord doesn't answer is because He has a wonderful answer, a comforting answer, a rejoicing answer, and He says, 'Where do I put it? There is no place yet in your heart, in your mind for me to put the answer. But life will create a holding place for the answer. So be patient; in time it will come. I have recorded your prayers. I know your needs. I will answer it when the holding place has been created.'"[54]

You may yet need to gain experience, perspective, tolerance, compassion. You may yet need to anguish through a Gethsemane of your own before you can fully understand the answer your Father is holding in reserve just for you, having created a space for that answer. Should He give it before you are ready, it may not be an answer that will bless and lift and inspire. It may not be an answer that will bring you peace. And so, in His wisdom, He holds on

---

53 Jeffrey R. Holland, *Created for Greater Things* (Salt Lake City: Deseret Book, 2011).
54 S. Michael Wilcox, "Bread or Stones: Understanding the God We Pray To," Devotional Address Given at Brigham Young University–Hawaii, March 31, 2009.

to it; with His infinite patience, He waits for *you*. For in this eternal kind of arithmetic, *you* are the quotient that determines the timetable.

Whatever you do while you are waiting for the answer, never stop praying. As Elder Jeffrey R. Holland counsels, "God is eagerly waiting for the chance to answer your prayers and fulfill your dreams, just as He always has. But He can't if you don't pray, and He can't if you don't dream. In short, He can't if you don't believe."[55]

How important it is that you believe in and trust God's timing. Think again of those Saints fleeing for their lives. Only months later—and for some, years later—did they receive the answers to their prayers for safety and peace. But the answers came. Perhaps some of them were like some of us, questioning God's timing against our own desperate need.

Elder Neal A. Maxwell said that faith in God must include trust in His timing.[56] He wrote, "The issue for us is trusting God enough to trust also His timing. If we can truly believe He has our welfare at heart, may we not let His plans unfold as He thinks best?"[57]

BYU religion professor Brad Wilcox cautions that just because we have to wait for an answer does not mean an answer is not coming. "Most of us agree that God is reliable and dependable, but our limited view makes us question His timing," he writes. "We sing, 'Jesus, Savior, pilot me' (*Hymns*, no. 104), but we still want to file our own flight plan and direct every takeoff and landing according to our schedule. God views all things—including time—differently than we do (see Alma 40:8). His delays are not denials."[58]

When we are met with this kind of dilemma, we come face-to-face with a singular predicament. We trust that God knows and understands us, even to the very depths of our heart and soul. Now it is incumbent on us to know and understand God, to see for perhaps the first time why He does what He does.

In his devotional address at BYU–Hawaii, S. Michael Wilcox explained our "need to understand something about our Father in Heaven, and that is that He is a fourth watch God."[59]

55 Jeffrey R. Holland, "This, the Greatest of All Dispensations," *Ensign*, July 2007.
56 Neal A. Maxwell, "Lest Ye Be Wearied and Faint in Your Minds," *Ensign*, May 1991.
57 Neal A. Maxwell, *Even As I Am* (Salt Lake City: Deseret Book, 1982), 93.
58 Brad Wilcox, *Changed through His Grace* (Salt Lake City: Deseret Book, 2017).
59 This and the following taken from S. Michael Wilcox, "Bread or Stones: Understanding the God We Pray To," Devotional Address Given at Brigham Young University–Hawaii, March 31, 2009.

Fourth watch? The Hebrew night was divided into four watches. The first watch was six to nine p.m.; the second watch was nine p.m. to midnight; the third watch was midnight to three a.m. The fourth watch—the very darkest and seemingly longest stretch of the night—was three a.m. to sunrise.

An episode in the sixth chapter of Mark demonstrates. It had been a long day—the day the Savior, moved with compassion toward a multitude that hungered, had fed five thousand men with five loaves of bread and two fishes: "And they did all eat, and were filled" (Mark 6:42).

Late that afternoon, He wanted to find a place of solitude where He could pray. He sent His disciples onto the Sea of Galilee in a boat, promising to meet them a little later on the shore, where they would pick Him up. After dismissing the multitudes who followed Him, He went into the surrounding mountains to seek His Father in prayer.

As the Savior was in the mountains praying, His disciples were facing a sore trial, likely symbolic of some of the painful burdens you have faced—or might be facing now. A ferocious wind began to sweep across the water, threatening the safety of the disciples and making it blisteringly difficult for them to row against the squall. Still the Savior prayed, we are told, late into the night.

Ever watching for Him, the disciples continued to row with all their might just to maintain their position in the sea. By the time they saw Him, they had rowed the equivalent of seventy-five football fields and were at the very end of their endurance. We read, "And He saw them toiling in rowing; for the wind was contrary unto them: and about the fourth watch of the night he cometh unto them, walking upon the sea" (Mark 6:48).

There are times in all of our lives when we too toil, rowing with all our might against the wind, even to the very last shred of our endurance. There are certainly times when we feel the forces against us are too powerful—that despite our best efforts, we will not be able to overcome a trial or we will not be able to see the fulfillment of a much-desired blessing.

In those desperate times, the muscles of your body and spirit weary from your frantic rowing, you might make certain dangerous assumptions. The first might be that He is not there, and that's why He isn't responding. But as you regain some calm, you know that isn't it. He is there. He is always there.

Then you fear that though He may be there, He must not be listening. That can't be it, because He *is* listening. He always listens. Remember the assurance of Elder Holland? *He hears your prayers.*[60] There is never a time

60 Jeffrey R. Holland, *Created for Greater Things* (Salt Lake City: Deseret Book, 2011).

when He fails to listen—never a time when your impassioned cries, sent heavenward on the tendrils of a heartfelt prayer, fail to reach His heart.

If He hears your prayers, then, and answers still don't come, you may feel that He doesn't care. Oh, He cares. He cares more than we can ever comprehend. President Dieter F. Uchtdorf assured, "He loves every one of us, even those who are flawed, rejected, awkward, sorrowful, or broken."[61] Nor can He ever forget us. As President Henry B. Eyring says, "Whether or not you choose to keep your covenant to always remember Him, He always remembers you."[62]

So if He is there, and He is listening, and He cares, why aren't your prayers being answered? Perhaps it is because He is a fourth watch God,[63] and you have not yet reached your fourth watch. A fourth watch God, says Wilcox, is one "who tends to feel that it is good to let His children toil in rowing against the wind to face a little opposition."[64] Or, as Elder Maxwell wrote, "God, as a loving Father, will stretch our souls at times. The soul is like a violin string: it makes music only when it is stretched. . . . God will tutor us by trying us because He loves us, not because of indifference!"[65]

The scriptures abound with fourth watch stories. Remember Joseph Smith in the Sacred Grove? As Joseph wrestled with the astonishing powers of darkness, "at the very moment when I was ready to sink into despair and abandon myself to destruction"—just at what he called "this moment of great alarm"—the Father and the Son arrived, and "I saw a pillar of light" (JS–H 1:16). They did not come when first he dropped to his knees. They did not arrive when he first posed the question that altered all eternity. No, They arrived at the fourth watch—at the moment of greatest despair, of darkest struggle.

Most of us are first watch people; we *want* our answers during the first watch. But we "worship a fourth watch God," Wilcox says. "So when the trials aren't over and the blessings don't come, don't assume that He is not there, or He is not listening, or He doesn't care, or you're not worthy. Always assume you have not yet reached the fourth watch."[66]

---

61 Dieter F. Uchtdorf, "The Love of God," *Ensign, Nov. 2009.*
62 Henry B. Eyring, "Always," *Ensign, Oct. 1999.*
63 S. Michael Wilcox, "Bread or Stones: Understanding the God We Pray To," Devotional Address Given at Brigham Young University–Hawaii, March 31, 2009.
64 Ibid.
65 Neal A. Maxwell, *All These Things Shall Give Thee Experience* (Salt Lake City: Deseret Book, 1979), 28.
66 S. Michael Wilcox, "Bread or Stones: Understanding the God We Pray To," Devotional Address Given at Brigham Young University–Hawaii, March 31, 2009.

What if you have been battered and bruised and scattered to the ends of your endurance? What if you're sure you're well past the fourth watch—what then?

> What we need to understand about our Father in Heaven is that He prefers to prepare us to face the storms of life, the contrary winds, rather than to still them. So if you are past your fourth watch and He has not come, don't assume that He is not there, that He doesn't care, He doesn't listen, or that you are not worthy. . . . You will not sink. Somewhere in the past of your life, experiences have been placed by a wise and foresighted Father in Heaven to prepare you to face the very things that you are facing. As the lion and the bear came to David, before Goliath, to prepare him to face Goliath, so will lion-and-bear moments come in your lives before the Goliath moments come. Because if . . . you have reached the fourth watch, He will come to you and still the storm.[67]

In other words, He will come. He will always come. Just as you are ready to give up, He will be there. And at that transcendent moment, as He comes to you as if walking across the sea, all will be made right again. You will know beyond any doubt that it was worth the wait.

Whatever you do, says Elder Holland, don't give up. "Don't give up when the pressure mounts. Certainly don't give in to that being who is bent on the destruction of your happiness. Face your doubts. Master your fears. 'Cast not away therefore your confidence.' Stay the course and see the beauty of life unfold for you."[68]

So as you pour out your heart to Him, trust Him. Trust His timing. And trust His answers. Wherever you are in this tutoring experience known as mortality, know that when you reach the edge of the cliff at the bitter end of your fourth watch you can step out into the darkness, being assured that either He will catch you or you will be taught how to fly.

---

67 Ibid.
68 Jeffrey R. Holland, "Cast Not Away Therefore Your Confidence," *Ensign*, Mar. 2000.

"LORD, HELP THOU MINE UNBELIEF"

Realizing The Savior's Atonement Is for You

> *"Everything in the gospel teaches us that we can change if*
> *we need to, that we can be helped if we truly want it,*
> *that we can be made whole, whatever the*
> *problems of the past."*
> —Elder Jeffrey R. Holland[69]

CHANCES ARE GOOD THAT YOU believe those words—that you truly believe that help is available, whatever the problems of the past.

There's a chance, though, that you believe those words apply to *everybody else.* But not to you.

Because it just might be that you also believe that the Atonement—the Savior's ultimate gift, His payment of the demands of justice, that thing He did for mankind because of His love, compassion, and grace—can work for everyone else . . . but that somehow it just won't work for *you.*

After all, you may reason, you've gone too far. You've missed too many chances. And now it is too late. Or you may think that because of some unfathomable ruse, you simply aren't covered by what took place in Gethsemane and on Calvary.

Oh, but you are. We *all* are. No matter what.

President Dieter F. Uchtdorf teaches, "[Jesus Christ] is the Savior and Redeemer of the world. He is the promised Messiah. He lived a perfect life and atoned for our sins. He will ever be at our side. He will fight our battles. He is our hope; He is our salvation; He is the way."[70]

He atoned for *our* sins. He is *our* hope. He is *our* salvation. Nowhere in that divinely inspired statement does an Apostle of the Lord say that He

69 Jeffrey R. Holland, *Created for Greater Things* (Salt Lake City: Deseret Book, 2011).
70 Dieter F. Uchtdorf, "The Way of the Disciple," *Ensign,* May 2009.

atoned for only *some of us.* That He is the hope for only *certain ones.* That He is the salvation for *a select group, but not all.*

No. Jesus Christ is all those things for *all of us.* And that includes *you.* It includes *you,* no matter what.

Christ received an assignment from our Heavenly Father to save *your* soul. *Yours* not by number, but by *name.* Christ knows you and loves you and willingly promised to do His very best to bring you back into the presence of the Father. That means even if you are at "rock bottom" and in your most wretched state, He is willing to come to you if you seek Him. His work and His glory is to bring to pass *your* immortality and eternal life. There are no more loving or capable hands than those who will reach to lift *you.*

Elder Jeffrey R. Holland said, "The world around us is an increasingly hostile and sinful place. Occasionally that splashes onto us, and perhaps, in the case of a few of you, it may be nearly drowning you. To anyone struggling under the burden of sin, I say again with the Prophet Joseph that God has 'a forgiving disposition' (*Lectures on Faith,* 42). You can change. You can be helped. *You can be made whole—whatever the problem.*"[71]

C. S. Lewis put it beautifully when he wrote that Christ "has infinite attention to spare for each one of us. He does not have to deal with us in the mass. You are as much alone with Him as if you were the only being He had ever created. *When Christ died, He died for you individually just as much as if you had been the only [person] in the world.*"[72]

Does that sound like you are in any way excluded from the Savior's great atoning sacrifice?

Absolutely not.

You never would be. Never could be.

On another occasion, C. S. Lewis summed it up even more powerfully: "He died not for men, but for each man. If each man had been the only man made, He would have done no less."[73]

And so, you think, that may be true—but maybe you have simply gone beyond the pale, are now in an untenable situation that puts you beyond the power of His Atonement.

Not so.

71 Jeffrey R. Holland, "Come Unto Me," *Ensign,* Apr. 1998, emphasis added; adapted from a CES Young Adult Fireside given at BYU on March 2, 1997.
72 C. S. Lewis, *Mere Christianity* (New York: HarperCollins, 2001); emphasis added.
73 Peter Kreeft, *C. S. Lewis for the Third Millennium: Six Essays on the Abolition of Man* (San Francisco: Ignatius Press, 1994), 217.

Elder Jeffrey R. Holland affirms, "However late you think you are, however many chances you think you have missed, however many mistakes you feel you have made or talents you think you don't have, or however far from home and family and God you feel you have traveled, I testify that you have *not* traveled beyond the reach of divine love. It is *not possible* for you to sink lower than the infinite light of Christ's Atonement shines."[74]

Not possible. So that is a worry you can cast aside with confidence, because a special witness of the Lord Jesus Christ has given you that assurance.

When it comes right down to it, you and I and all the rest of us are really in a difficult position because it is utterly impossible for us to fully understand the Atonement of Jesus Christ. We are in a mortal sphere, possessed of temporal minds with finite understanding. Some things we *do* know. We know of the unsurpassed importance of His Atonement. Elder Tad R. Callister wrote, "The Atonement of Jesus Christ outweighs, surpasses, and transcends every other mortal event, every new discovery, and every acquisition of knowledge, for without the Atonement all else in life is meaningless."[75]

Even knowing and understanding that, we are still not fully capable of grasping exactly how it works. This is where trust comes in. President Dieter F. Uchtdorf helped clarify that when he said, "The one help we all need is given to us freely through the Atonement of Jesus Christ. Having faith in Jesus Christ and in His Atonement means relying completely on Him—trusting in His infinite power, intelligence, and love."[76]

We may not understand exactly *how* it happened, but we do know *where* it happened. Leaving His three most trusted disciples by the garden gate, Christ entered Gethsemane, a grove of olive trees on the Mount of Olives. "And he went a little further, and fell on his face, and prayed, saying, O my Father, if it be possible, let this cup pass from me" (Matthew 26:39). With those words, there can be no doubt in your mind that He knew exactly what a grueling thing He was about to experience.

But there can also be no doubt in your mind that He would never fail at what He had been called to do, because He finished His simple prayer by uttering, ". . . nevertheless, not as I will, but as thou wilt" (Matthew 26:39).

---

74 Jeffrey R. Holland, "The Laborers in the Vineyard," *Ensign*, May 2012; emphasis added.

75 Tad R. Callister, *The Infinite Atonement* (Salt Lake City: Deseret Book, 2000).

76 Dieter F. Uchtdorf, "Christlike Attributes—the Wind Beneath Our Wings," *Ensign*, Nov. 2005.

Twice as His ordeal was beginning, He returned to the garden gate to find His disciples sleeping, "for their eyes were heavy" (Matthew 26:43). Twice He woke them, pleading with them to watch with Him for even an hour. With willing spirits but weak flesh, they again fell asleep. And then came the anguished hour that marked the beginning of His staggering sacrifice for you. For me. For all of us.

Elder Holland paints for us a poignant view of what happened next in that garden:

> In that most burdensome moment of all human history, with blood appearing at every pore and an anguished cry upon His lips, Christ sought Him whom He had always sought—His Father. 'Abba,' He cried, 'Papa,' or from the lips of a younger child, 'Daddy.' This is such a personal moment it almost seems a sacrilege to cite it. A Son in un-relieved pain, a Father His only true source of strength, both of them staying the course, making it through the night—together.[77]

Once the everlasting sacrifice began, the Son—He who bled from every pore as He paid the price for every sin that would ever be committed—never even remotely entertained the thought of failing to follow through. No notion of backing out ever crossed His glorious mind. And for all of His distress in watching His Only Begotten Son suffering as no mortal had ever suffered, the Father also stayed the course. How inconsolably wrenching it must have been for Him to watch His Beloved Son in such torment. Together, though, they prevailed—guaranteed that no one who ever wanted to return, who took advantage of His Atonement, would be denied. *No one.* Including you. Your name was on His lips as He made sure you would have a way.

There is no way to fully comprehend what happened that night in Gethsemane. Elder Keith R. Edwards said, "We can never endure the depth, the exquisite nature, or the magnitude of His suffering, 'which suffering caused myself, even God, the greatest of all, to tremble because of pain, and to bleed at every pore, and to suffer both body and spirit' (D&C 19:18). But . . . we can have a greater appreciation for that which He did, and we can feel

---

77 Jeffrey R. Holland, "The Hands of the Fathers," *Ensign*, May 1999.

His spirit succoring us, and we can know the Savior in a very real sense."[78] And, after all, "this is life eternal, that [you] might know" Him (John 17:3).

From Gethsemane, the Savior was taken to Caiaphas's Palace, where He was subjected to the indignity of a mock trial. Crowned with plaited thorns and whipped beyond any mortal's ability to survive, He was driven along the path to a hill overlooking the highway, forced to carry the cross upon which He would be crucified.

With nails driven through His palms, wrists, and feet, He hung in agony while the world groaned at His misery. During those hours on the cross, undergoing the most painful death that could be exacted at that time, He once again took on every sin and sickness and sorrow that could ever beset any mortal. And once again, your name was on His lips as He felt overwhelming love for you. Can you grasp the magnitude of that—of His going through that astonishing suffering a second time? With it, there can be *no doubt* that everyone is included. There is *no way* that anyone fell through the cracks. He covered us all, every single one. His torture ended only when He declared, "Father, into thy hands I commend my spirit: and having said thus, he gave up the ghost" (Luke 23:46).

It was finished. And in its magnificent calculation, it covered every person ever created in every world. *Every person.* Including *you.* There was never a moment when you were ever excluded from the triumph that was His.

But it really wasn't finished. Not quite. He had promised to come again in three days to rise again, the first fruits of all those who slept (see 1 Corinthians 15:20). It's almost impossible to imagine the feelings that filled the heart of the faithful Mary Magdalene when she arrived at His grave that Sunday morning only to find it empty. Seeing the Savior standing outside His sepulcher, she didn't recognize Him at first, but thought He was the gardener.

Of course. We would all probably think the same thing. After all, she had watched His lifeless body as it was removed from the cross. Had accompanied it to the garden tomb. Had watched the massive stone rolled to guard the entrance. Had shed bitter tears for the loss of someone so dear to her.

When at once she recognized Him, she moved toward Him with what must have been a combination of astonishment and joy. At that moment,

---

78 Keith R. Edwards, "That They Might Know Thee," *Ensign*, Nov. 2006.

the Savior told her, "Touch me not, for I am not yet ascended to my Father: but go to my brethren, and say unto them, I ascend unto my Father, and your Father; and to my God, and your God" (John 20:17).

He had done what He had promised. He had broken the bands of death. In that singular act, your Savior and Redeemer made it possible for *all mankind* to be resurrected. That includes *you*. Never were you excluded from that miracle. He gave us—*all of us* who have ever lived—the gift of immortality.

Because the Atonement of Jesus Christ is so infinite in its scope, every one of us has access to it. But your ability to gain that access depends on you. Christ respects your agency. He will not come unless you call. He won't answer unless you knock.

I've always thought it curious that He makes *us* seek *Him*. He already knows where we are, how we are, what we've done, and what we're doing. He knows every intent of our hearts, often before we do. But it is by seeking Him that we activate the first part of His Atonement, which allows us to have a direct link to Him. It's that simple and that wonderful. We all have the right and even the *responsibility* to seek the Savior. Through life's experiences I've come to believe that He requires us to seek Him to prove our own desires, humility, and readiness for what happens when we find Him.

So how can you seek Him? Prayer is the initial way. Satan wants to shove you off the edge of the mountain, causing you to plummet to the rocks below. He wants to destroy you. The Lord warned us: "What I say unto one I say unto all; pray always lest that wicked one have power in you, and remove you out of your place" (D&C 93:49). In those words is the key: Pray. Pray *always*. Dig in your heels, and refuse to be removed from your place.

Your ability to cling to the Savior of all mankind is made possible by His Atonement. And oh, how critical it is. Have you ever emerged from a dramatic, chaotic situation and thought, *I did everything I could, and it wasn't enough?* That's because everything *you* can do *isn't* enough. It's only enough when *your* everything joins with *Christ's* everything.

In our Herculean efforts, we mortals find that we are only human after all. On our own, we have not been self-reliant at all, but have turned our power over to the adversary. The only way to get it back is to turn it over once again—to our Advocate, He who atoned for us in every possible way.

The Atonement of Jesus Christ brings with it two remarkable gifts. One—the one we most often consider—gives us the ability to repent. For every mistake or error or sin, there is a price: restitution must be made, consequences paid. Those are the demands of justice, and we know that our God is a just God.

But we also know that our God is a merciful God, and so He paved the way for someone else to pay the price of all our sins if we would but repent. Very realistically, it's like this: Imagine that you commit a crime; you are arrested, tried, and convicted, required to exact the punishment prescribed. At the last minute, someone steps up and says, "No, don't send her. Send me. I will serve her sentence." And with that, you are free.

The sublime news is that you *are* free because someone—Jesus Christ, your Savior and Redeemer—has *already paid the price* and accepted the "punishment" for every wrong you can ever commit. He did it in the garden and on the cross. It has already been accomplished. It is now up to you to accept that incredible gift—to take advantage of what He did for you. What He did specifically and directly for *you.*

As you exercise His Atonement in your life, you can literally cast your "care upon him; for he careth for [you]" (1 Peter 5:7).

Elder Ronald E. Poelman teaches, "When we disobey the laws of God, justice requires that compensation be made—a requirement which we are incapable of fulfilling. But out of His divine love for us, our Father has provided a plan and a Savior, Jesus Christ, whose redeeming sacrifice satisfies the demands of justice for us and makes possible repentance, forgiveness, and reconciliation with our Father."[79]

Because of the Savior's Atonement, "He who has repented of his sins, the same is forgiven, and I, the Lord, remember them no more" (D&C 58:42).

The ability to be forgiven of your sins through the Savior's Atonement is one of the greatest sources of peace and comfort you can ever experience in mortality. One of the most powerful dialogues in all of scripture was the one in which Alma the Younger described to his son Helaman the "inexpressible horror" he felt as he imagined coming into the presence of God to be judged for his many transgressions (see Alma 36:14).

Thinking about his sins, Alma wished that he "could be banished and become extinct both soul and body, that I might not be brought to stand in the presence of my God, to be judged of my deeds." His misery lasted for "three days and three nights" as he was "racked, even with the pains of a damned soul" (Alma 36:15–16). Crying out to Jesus, whom he knew to

79 Ronald E. Poelman, "God's Love for Us Transcends Our Transgressions," *Ensign*, May 1982.

be the Son of God, he described himself as "in the gall of bitterness" and as being "encircled about by the everlasting chains of death" (Alma 36:18).

As if by a miracle, Alma could remember his sins no more. "And oh, what joy, and what marvelous light did I behold; yea, my soul was filled with joy as exceeding as was my pain! Yea, I say unto you, my son, that there could be nothing so exquisite and so bitter as were my pains. Yea, and again I say unto you, my son, that on the other hand, there can be nothing so exquisite and sweet as was my joy" (Alma 36:20–21).

As he described it firsthand to his son, Alma said that *nothing was so exquisite and sweet as the joy of having been forgiven.* Now, instead of dreading the prospect of facing God, battered and soiled with sin, he saw in vision God sitting upon His throne, and "my soul did long to be there" (Alma 36:22).

Christ's suffering for you in Gethsemane and on the cross at Calvary makes it possible for you to feel that same exquisite joy as you repent and are forgiven of any wrongdoings in your life. As you do, you are given that sublime promise: "I, the Lord, remember them no more" (D&C 58:42). Because of those hours in which He exacted His Atonement, the price is paid, and you are free.

All of holy writ testifies of what took place for you. Isaiah testified, "He hath borne our griefs, and carried our sorrows . . . He was wounded for our transgressions, he was bruised for our iniquities: . . . and with his stripes we are healed" (Isaiah 53:4–5). And the Lord Himself declared, "I, God, have suffered these things for all, that they might not suffer if they would repent" (D&C 19:16).

He agonized for *you* so that you can be spared that torment. If you will but repent, He has already done the suffering. Paid the price. And now He opens His arms and invites you in. Elder Neil L. Andersen said, "I have thought of the Lord's invitation to come unto Him and to spiritually be wrapped in His arms. He said, 'Behold, [my arms] of mercy [are] extended towards you, and *whosoever will come, him will I receive*; and blessed are those who come unto me' (3 Nephi 9:14; emphasis added)."[80]

Whosoever will come. Not just the special ones. Not just the ones with impressive callings or big houses or movie-star good looks. Not just the smart or the rich or the famous. Them, of course, but everyone else. *Whosoever.* Whatever person. You, and me.

80 Neil L. Andersen, "Repent . . . That I May Heal You," *Ensign*, Nov. 2009.

The scriptures, say Elder Andersen, constantly remind us that the Savior's arms are open (see Mormon 6:17). Stretched out (see 2 Kings 17:36). Extended (see Alma 19:36). Encircling (see 2 Nephi 1:15). Those arms that were once nailed to a cross are now arms of mercy (see Alma 5:33). Arms of safety (see Alma 34:16). Arms that are mighty and holy (see 3 Nephi 20:35). Arms that are "lengthened out all the day long" (see 2 Nephi 28:32)—for *you*. To hold you and shelter you against all that sin might exact on you. Instead, wrapped in His spiritual arms, you will feel His forgiveness, His love, and His comfort.

Ultimately, there is only one enduring source of comfort: He who suffered for you. Elder Richard G. Scott testified, "Jesus Christ paid the price and satisfied the demands of justice for all who are obedient to His teachings. Thus, full forgiveness is granted, and the distressing effects of sin need no longer persist in one's life. Indeed, they *cannot persist* if one truly understands the meaning of Christ's Atonement."[81]

But comfort is only the beginning. With the power of His Atonement, you are given the precious gift of becoming better than you could possibly become on your own. President Henry B. Eyring taught, "The Spirit not only comforts you, but He is also the agent by which the Atonement works a change in your very nature."[82] Elder David A. Bednar said that "the enabling and strengthening aspect of the Atonement helps us to see and to do and to become good in ways that we could never recognize or accomplish with our limited mortal capacity. I testify and witness that the enabling power of the Savior's Atonement is real."[83]

What if you take the steps to repent but fail to feel the promised comfort? Does that mean your original premise was right—that the Savior's Atonement may work for others, but not for you?

No.

It means only that there is a process and a healing that must take place. The promised comfort is sure and, unlike some playground games, it excludes no one. Elder Andersen counseled, "As we honestly confess our sins, restore what we can to the offended, and forsake our sins by keeping the commandments, we are in the *process* of receiving forgiveness. *With time*, we will feel the anguish of our sorrow subside, taking 'away the guilt

81 Richard G. Scott, "We Love You—Please Come Back," *Ensign*, May 1986.
82 Henry B. Eyring, "My Peace I Leave with You," *Ensign*, May 2017.
83 David A. Bednar, "In the Strength of the Lord," *Ensign*, Nov. 2004.

from our hearts' (Alma 24:10) and bringing 'peace of conscience' (Mosiah 4:3). For those who are truly repentant but seem unable to feel relief: continue keeping the commandments. I promise you, *relief will come in the timetable of the Lord.* Healing also requires time."[84] He who knows all knows the timetable best suited for your heart.

In addition to offering the opportunity to repent, there is another sublime aspect of the Savior's Atonement that is sometimes overlooked. The Savior Himself offers you an extraordinary invitation: "Come unto me, all ye that labor and are heavy laden, and I will give you rest. Take my yoke upon you, and learn of me; for I am meek and lowly in heart: and ye shall find rest unto your souls. For my yoke is easy, and my burden is light" (Matthew 11:28–30).

Once you really grasp the meaning of those simple words, their message is clear: you no longer have to suffer from *any* burden—not sin, not grief, not betrayal, not illness—because the Savior, through His Atonement, will give you rest.

Perhaps you feel reluctant to place any more burden on Christ than you already contributed to His suffering in Gethsemane. Maybe you worry that with the magnitude of what He has already taken on, you should not encumber Him with your comparatively insignificant hardships. *Certainly if you try hard enough and work diligently enough, you can cope with the agonies you are facing.*

Oh, but that's not how it works. Through some divine formula, placing your burdens at His feet adds not an ounce to what He is already carrying for all of us. Pleading for His caring concern and healing help is no imposition on Him, nor could it ever be; He *wants* us to respond to His invitation. He wants to give us *rest unto our souls,* now and forever.

And the Savior's promise to give you rest is real. It is there for you because, as He explains, He will never forget you: "Behold, I have graven thee upon the palms of my hands; thy walls are continually before me" (1 Nephi 21:16).

What does it mean to have you graven upon the palms of His hands? It means that the "Lord loves you. He knows your hopes and your disappointments. He will not forget you because your pains and your suffering are continually before Him."[85] It means "there is One who does

84 Neil L. Andersen, "Repent . . . That I May Heal You," *Ensign,* Nov. 2009; emphasis added.
85 Silvia Allred, "Steadfast and Immovable," *Ensign,* Nov. 2010.

[fully understand]. He knows. He has felt your pain. . . . The Savior is there, reaching out to *each of us*, bidding us: 'Come unto me' (3 Nephi 9:14)."[86]

Because you are graven upon His hands, you can be assured that He understands all your sorrows and pain and sickness and anguish. For all that you suffer, no matter its source, Jesus can lift your burdens because, in some unfathomable way, He bore them long before you did.

In Gethsemane, writhing against anguish that is completely unimaginable to us, He suffered "pains and afflictions and temptations of every kind; and this that the word might be fulfilled which saith *he will take upon him the pains and the sicknesses of his people*. And he will take upon him death, that he may loose the bands of death which bind his people; and he will take upon him their infirmities, that his bowels may be filled with mercy, according to the flesh, *that he may know according to the flesh how to succor his people according to their infirmities*" (Alma 7:11–12; emphasis added).

The Lord went through the agony of Gethsemane not only to pay the price for your sins, but to literally *experience* every pain and sickness and infirmity and sorrow and betrayal and anguish you would ever feel. He did it so He could *succor* you—a word that means "to run to the rescue."[87] *To run*. Not wander. Not approach with hesitation. Not get around to when He has nothing better to do. He stands by, waiting to *run to your rescue*, no matter what you are suffering. He is uniquely qualified to do that, because He suffered it before you.

He knows how it feels to be betrayed by an unfaithful husband. He knows how it feels to lose a baby. He knows how it feels to battle breast cancer. He knows how it feels to worry over a child who has lost the way. He knows all that, because He experienced it all there in a grove of olive trees in the black of a night that changed the course of eternity. You are one of them to whom it was promised: "They shall hunger no more, neither thirst any more; neither shall the sun light on them, nor any heat. For the Lamb which is in the midst of the throne shall feed them, and shall lead them unto living fountains of waters: and *God shall wipe away all tears from their eyes*" (Revelation 7:16–17; emphasis added).

It is through the Atonement of Jesus Christ that ultimately all losses can be restored, all suffering can cease, and all inequities and injustices can

86 Neil L. Andersen, "Repent . . . That I May Heal You," *Ensign*, Nov. 2009; emphasis added.
87 Jeffrey R. Holland, "Come unto Me" (Brigham Young University fireside, March 2, 1997), 9, speeches.byu.edu.

be rectified. You are not guaranteed a life free from pain, worry, heartache, sickness, and adversity. But when you rely on the Savior's Atonement, *you are guaranteed a sure arrival home.*

"LORD, MAKE ME WHOLE"

Discovering the Miracle of Forgiveness

> *"To be a Christian means to forgive the inexcusable in others because God has forgiven the inexcusable in you."*
> —C. S. Lewis[88]

FORGIVENESS. IT'S A WORD, A concept that most often brings up images of Jesus Christ writhing in agony in Gethsemane, paying the ultimate sacrifice so you can be forgiven of your sins. Made clean. Made whole. Able to approach the judgment bar with a conscience clear of offense.

And that is exactly what you are offered by the Savior of all mankind—a gift so remarkable it is almost beyond comprehension. It erases every wrong. It is one of the greatest sources of hope imaginable. It makes all things possible, here and hereafter.

Elder Jeffrey R. Holland summed it up eloquently when he wrote to those who may feel broken and battered by the extremities of life's experiences:

> To all of you who think you are lost or without hope, or who think you have done too much that was too wrong for too long, to every one of you who worry that you are stranded somewhere on the wintry plains of life and have wrecked your handcart in the process, we call out Jehovah's unrelenting refrain, '[My] hand is stretched out still' (see Isaiah 5:25; 9:17, 21). . . . His mercy endureth forever,

88 C. S. Lewis, *The Weight of Glory* (New York: Harper Collins, 2001; originally published in 1949).

and His hand is stretched out still. His is the pure love of Christ, the charity that never faileth, that compassion which endures even when all other strength disappears.[89]

Every one of us is a beggar before God. Even you. You will certainly remember humbly approaching your Heavenly Father at some point in your life, pleading for the mercy made possible by the Savior's divine Atonement. You will certainly remember an occasion when you begged to be forgiven of a mistake you made—or even a more serious sin you committed. Reflecting on those times, you will remember that forgiveness came. That your Father remembered your sin no more.

You know the same thing will happen each time you approach Him with that request.

Every time.

You are assured. His hand is stretched out still. His compassion for you endures, even when all else in your life seems lost or hopeless. You need never be defined by the mistakes you have made. There is forevermore a chance to start over. A clean slate.

That forgiveness, of course, comes with conditions—not just for you, but for all of us.

First of all, you need to repent. You *know* you can do that. After all, you've been tutored by the best—the Savior who paid the price to make your repentance possible. You know the steps. You are probably exercised in taking your deepest regrets to Him who will wash them away and restore your peace—to Him who will always be at your side when all others have abandoned you.

But there is another condition on the Savior's gift to you.

You must forgive others.

And while you are able to plead with the Lord for forgiveness of *your* sins, this other condition may prove much more difficult. In some cases—situations in which you have been wronged beyond comprehension—it may be too daunting to even consider.

Can there be no other way?

There is not. The Lord is clear on the requirement: "I, the Lord, will forgive whom I will forgive, but of you it is required to forgive all men" (D&C 64:10). *All.* Not just the ones who have committed the smaller offenses, whose insults seem slight. Not just the ones who are easiest to

---

89 Jeffrey R. Holland, *Broken Things to Mend* (Salt Lake City: Deseret Book, 2008).

forgive. Not just the ones who are kind and loving and forgiving in return. *All.*

Even the one who has inflicted a wound so deep that you fear you will never heal again. Even that one.

President Dieter F. Uchtdorf has this to say about the Savior's command: "Our Savior has spoken so clearly on this subject that there is little room for private interpretation."[90] On another occasion, President Uchtdorf clarified the Savior's words with his own: "Each of us is under a divinely spoken obligation to reach out with pardon and mercy and to forgive one another."[91] Another modern-day Apostle wrote a similarly stirring injunction: "We don't want God to remember our sins, so there is something fundamentally wrong in our relentlessly trying to remember those of others."[92]

The Savior promised that any time we give, "it shall be given unto you . . . For with the same measure that [you use] it shall be measured to you again" (Luke 6:38). His words apply to all we would give. Including forgiveness. Simple: if you forgive, you will be forgiven. Measure for measure.

But what if it's just too hard?

What if the hurt was just too profound?

Forgiveness is not a simple concept. It means that you grant pardon. That you release your claim on someone else. That you free someone from blame or guilt or consequences for whatever that person did to you. That you cancel any liability. And maybe most difficult of all, that you cease to feel resentment toward the one you forgive.

You certainly hope that your Heavenly Father does all of those things in *your* behalf when it is you crying on your knees in your secret places for His complete forgiveness. But when *you* are required to do the same thing for those who may have brutally betrayed you in the most heinous way, there is nothing easy or simple about it.

Nothing.

While there is nothing easy about it, our willingness to forgive is undeniably linked to our ability to be forgiven by the Savior. President Uchtdorf put it this way: "Because we all depend on the mercy of God, how can we deny to others any measure of the grace we so desperately desire for ourselves? . . . [S]hould we not forgive as we wish to be forgiven?"[93]

90 Dieter F. Uchtdorf, "The Merciful Obtain Mercy," *Ensign*, May 2012.
91 Dieter F. Uchtdorf, "Point of Safe Return," *Ensign*, May 2007.
92 Jeffrey R. Holland, *Created for Greater Things* (Salt Lake City: Deseret Book, 2011).
93 Dieter F. Uchtdorf, "The Merciful Obtain Mercy," *Ensign*, May 2012.

We are all mortals sharing a mortal experience, and there will always be those times when people do things that disappoint you, hurt you, or make you angry. That's just the way mortality is. Those things will be done to you. Don't forget the flip side: you will also do them to others. Certainly, there will be times when you may even wound or disappoint your Father in Heaven. He knows that and expects it, because He knows all things before they happen. When those things *do happen, He hopes you will come to Him in sorrow, expressing your remorse and begging for His divine forgiveness. And when you do, He grants that forgiveness without reservation. And be assured that nothing you can do will ever change His love for you.*

Why should you be any different? Yes, you are mortal. "We are not perfect. The people around us are not perfect," says President Uchtdorf. But recognize this: "[Forgiveness] is the Lord's way. Remember, heaven is filled with those who have this in common: They are forgiven. And they forgive."[94]

Heaven will not be filled with those who never made mistakes, but with those who recognized their wrongs, pleaded for forgiveness, and changed the choices they were making.

Yes, heaven will be filled with those who gained forgiveness. It will also be filled with those who forgave others—who walked as Christ walked, filled with His Spirit.

Perhaps you have been deeply hurt by someone who will never ask your forgiveness. Doesn't matter. You need to forgive anyway. Maybe your forgiveness will be a quiet, private change within the secret places of your heart—forgiveness granted but never even realized or acknowledged by the one you forgive. Doesn't matter. You need to forgive anyway. The only person in this equation you have any control over is *you.*

When you have forgiven, you need to put it away. For good. Resist the temptation to bring it out again and give it the airtime it needs to inhabit your heart all over again. Most important, don't use it against the person you forgave—because now *you* are the one who is causing hurt.

Elder Holland said, "*Let people repent. Let people grow. Believe that people can change and improve. . . . If something is buried in the past, leave it buried. Don't keep going back with your little sand pail and beach shovel to dig it up, wave it around, and then throw it at someone, saying, 'Hey! Do you remember*

---

94 Ibid.

this?' Splat!"[95] When you leave the grievance or the hurt or the betrayal buried, the benefit isn't limited to the person you forgive. You benefit too. As President Uchtdorf explains, we "will receive the joy of forgiveness in our own lives when we are willing to extend that joy freely to others. . . . As a result, the Spirit of the Lord will fill our souls with the joy accompanying divine peace of conscience (see Mosiah 4:2–3)."[96]

Look at what happens when someone devastates you—crushes you so harshly that you worry you will never be the same again. For a while, you aren't. Because suddenly a hefty piece of real estate in your heart has been shattered, letting in feelings of resentment and anger and maybe even hatred. Those feelings threaten to take up permanent residence in your exhausted and battered heart, crowding out feelings of love and peace and acceptance.

At first, the thought of forgiving that person threatens you in a very real way. Not only do you find it staggeringly impossible; you also resist giving up those pieces of your heart that have now found shelter. You may not even *like* them, but they are part of you now.

But when you take the risk—when you accept the Savior's invitation to follow Him—those spaces in your heart that were filled with resentment and anger are healed. Anger and resentment and even hatred are banished, and the spaces that used to shelter them are gloriously opened, creating space for love and joy. Creating space for the Spirit.

You move forward in faith, taking those initial shaky steps that at first seem so difficult. Almost impossible. As you do, you experience a mighty change of heart—exactly what your relationship with Jesus Christ is meant to bring into your life.

So how can it be done?

One thing that can pave the way to forgiveness is to seek understanding. "Too often we look at the offender the way we would look at an iceberg— we only see the tip and not beneath the surface," says Elder Kevin R. Duncan. "We do not know all that is going on in a person's life. We do not know their past; we do not know their struggles; we do not know the pains they carry."[97]

---

95 Jeffrey R. Holland, "'Remember Lot's Wife': Faith Is for the Future," *Brigham Young University Speeches*, Jan 13, 2009; in "The Best Is Yet to Be," *Ensign*, Jan. 2010.
96 Dieter F. Uchtdorf, "Point of Safe Return," *Ensign*, May 2007.
97 Kevin R. Duncan, "The Healing Ointment of Forgiveness," *Ensign*, May 2016.

One key to forgiving others, then, says Elder Duncan, "is to try to see them as God sees them. At times, God may part the curtain and bless us with the gift to see into the heart, soul, and spirit of another person who has offended us. This insight may even lead to an overwhelming love for that person."98

But what if you *know* that you are right and the other person is wrong? Are you just supposed to swallow the wrong? What if others—even the person you are trying to forgive—think *you* are the wrong one? Elder Lynn A. Mickelsen addressed exactly that when he said:

> The Lord has been clear in His instruction regarding this dilemma. It is not our prerogative to judge. The mote is not ours to measure, for the beam in our own eye obstructs our capacity to see. There is no pancake so thin it has only one side. Empathy is required here, the gift to feel what others feel and to understand what others are experiencing. Empathy is the natural outgrowth of charity. It stimulates and enhances our capacity to serve. Empathy is not sympathy but understanding and caring. It is the basis of true friendship. Empathy leads to respect and opens the door to teaching and learning. The Sioux Indians understand this great principle as they pray, "Great Spirit, help me to never judge another until I have walked for two weeks in his moccasins."99

In the most desperate of cases, you might need to forgive someone who is dangerous—who has literally put you in harm's way or who has injured you. What then? Are you still under the command to forgive?

Yes.

But in cases such as those, you are not expected to invite that person back into your life, subjecting you to the possibility of more harm. Elder Duncan clarified, "Please do not misunderstand. To forgive is not to condone. We do not rationalize bad behavior or allow others to mistreat us *because* of their struggles, pains, or weaknesses." But the process of

---

98 Ibid.
99 Lynn A. Mickelsen, "The Atonement, Repentance, and Dirty Linen," *Ensign*, Nov. 2003.

forgiveness in those cases, he says, allows us to "gain greater understanding and peace."[100]

In the end, the most certain way to forgive is through the love of God. President Uchtdorf promises, "The more we allow the love of God to govern our minds and emotions—the more we allow our love for our Heavenly Father to swell within our hearts—the easier it is to love others with the pure love of Christ."[101] Even those you might find it hard to forgive.

Even them.

When you involve the Savior in your every effort, you are invited to cast your burden at His feet. That includes the burden of a pain so piercing you fear it will never mend. Let Him help you, because He stands ready to do exactly that. Let His Atonement change your heart and heal your soul. Then let His Atonement help you reach out to heal another.

As President Uchtdorf counsels, "Love one another. Forgive one another. The merciful will obtain mercy."[102]

As you forgive, you extend to another what the Savior forever stands ready to extend to you. As Elder Dale G. Renlund said, "The Savior's mortal ministry was indeed characterized by love, compassion, and empathy. He did not disdainfully walk the dusty roads of Galilee and Judea, flinching at the sight of sinners. He did not dodge them in abject horror. No, He ate with them (see Luke 15:1–2). He helped and blessed, lifted and edified, and replaced fear and despair with hope and joy."[103]

As you forgive, that is yours to bestow.

---

100 Kevin R. Duncan, "The Healing Ointment of Forgiveness," *Ensign*, May 2016.
101 Dieter F. Uchtdorf, "The Merciful Obtain Mercy," *Ensign*, May 2012.
102 Ibid.
103 Dale G. Renlund, "Our Good Shepherd," *Ensign*, May 2017.

"LET NOT YOUR HEART BE TROUBLED"

Finding Peace and Comfort

> *"Peace I leave with you, my peace I give unto you:*
> *not as the world giveth, give I unto you.*
> *Let not your heart be troubled, neither let it be afraid."*
> —John 14:27

THE WORD *PEACE* OFTEN BRINGS to mind the state of the world—a hoped-for day in which all nations will cease warring and will live together in the kind of harmony we have been promised following the Savior's Second Coming. We look for the blessed day "when the lamb and the lion shall lie down together without any ire."[104]

As welcome as such a day will be, we are acutely aware that it is not yet here. We know of the calamities foretold by prophets since the beginning of time regarding our day—the "winding-up scene."[105] Our time is one that Elder Dallin H. Oaks calls "a time of turmoil. There are wars between some nations, armed conflicts within others, and violent controversies in most. *People are killed every day* in some places, and hatred is practiced in many more. Peace is a victim everywhere."[106]

It cannot have escaped your attention that there's not much you can do about wars between nations. Armed conflicts. Violent controversies. The adversary would actually have you focus on those "mists of darkness" that blind the eyes, harden the heart, and lead us away (see 1 Nephi 12:17). He would have you believe there is nothing you can do to achieve peace. He would have you give up. Have you resign yourself to a conflicted and

---

104 "The Spirit of God," *Hymns*, no. 2.
105 Russell M. Nelson, "A Plea to My Sisters," *Ensign*, Nov. 2015.
106 Dallin H. Oaks, "World Peace," *Ensign*, May 1990; emphasis added.

troubled existence, because then you would be far from the Spirit—and, having lost the comforting arm of the Spirit, far from divine assistance.

Abandoned, forced to make it on your own.

That's what he wants for you. Because he wants you to be "miserable like unto himself" (2 Nephi 2:27).

But there is another—One much more powerful—whose goal is your happiness. And He can help you achieve another, even more important kind of peace that *is well within your grasp:* inner peace, or peace of mind. Instead of driving away the Spirit, it invites the Spirit. Instead of abandoning you in heartache and distress, it lifts and heals.

Inner peace is a condition hallmarked by freedom from annoyance, distraction, anxiety, and obsession. It is characterized by stillness. Tranquility. Contentment. It is a deliberate state of spiritual calm that defies everything going on around you. It is part of what President Dieter F. Uchtdorf called "an astonishing wealth of light and truth"[107] that surrounds you even in this time of chaos and calamity.

It is your birthright. It is one of the sure weapons in your arsenal that will help you through whatever is happening around you and around the world.

Maybe you can't quite imagine feeling that kind of peace. Perhaps there is a situation—or, likely, more than just one—that harrows your thoughts and breaks your heart and has you convinced that you will never be at peace.

If peace has eluded you, listen to the marvelous message of hope the Apostle Paul shared with the Corinthians. He addressed a people who were troubled on every side, perplexed, persecuted, and even "cast down," as he described it. Not conditions conducive to inner peace. Yet here is what he wrote to those people, people who were perilously close to giving up: "We are troubled on every side, yet not distressed; we are perplexed, but not in despair; Persecuted, but not forsaken; cast down, but not destroyed" (2 Corinthians 4:8–9).

Those who read Paul's inspired epistle must have identified readily with his narrative of being troubled, perplexed, persecuted, and cast down. For reasons uniquely your own, you may have felt some of these same difficult emotions. What may *not* have been apparent to the Corinthians—or maybe to you—was Paul's description of feeling *not* distressed, *not* in despair, *not* forsaken, and *not* destroyed.

---

107 Dieter F. Uchtdorf, "O How Great the Plan of Our God!" *Ensign*, Nov. 2016.

What could have led Paul to that conclusion? It was something available to the Corinthians two thousand years ago and something that is available to you right now. It is the light of God, "who commanded the light to shine out of darkness"—a light that gives us the glory of God "in the face of Jesus Christ" (2 Corinthians 4:6).

The message is clear. If you are feeling troubled, fearful, anxious, worried, distressed, and even forsaken, there is a sure remedy. It is the Lord Jesus Christ, who declared, "Learn of me, and listen to my words; walk in the meekness of my Spirit, *and you shall have peace in me*" (D&C 19:23; emphasis added). Truly, His is the peace "which passeth all understanding" (Philippians 4:7).

The Savior's promise is clear and consistent. On the very night in which He agonized in a grove of olive trees at Gethsemane to give us all the greatest measure of hope imaginable, He told His fearful disciples, "Peace I leave with you, my peace I give unto you. . . . Let not your heart be troubled, neither let it be afraid" (John 14:27). He gives that same promise to all of us, we who were not with Him at that Last Supper. He gives it to you, no matter your circumstance—no matter the things that would combine to rob you of your inner peace.

Did you notice that commandment given by the Lord in that simple verse? "Let not your heart be troubled, neither let it be afraid." He was not speaking only to His disciples, but to all of us, even to our day. Of that mandate, Elder Jeffrey R. Holland wrote, "I submit to you, that may be one of the Savior's commandments that is, even in the hearts of otherwise faithful Latter-day Saints, almost universally disobeyed; and yet I wonder whether our resistance to this invitation could be any more grievous to the Lord's merciful heart."[108]

Elder Holland further taught, "Trumpeted from the summit of Calvary is the truth that we will never be left alone nor unaided, even if sometimes we may feel that we are. Truly the Redeemer of us all said: 'I will not leave you comfortless: [My Father and] I will come to you [and abide with you]' (John 14:18)."[109]

A well-known event in the Savior's life demonstrates both His resolve to comfort and the imperative all of us have in response to His efforts to bring us peace. The Savior's disciples had been waiting for Him in a ship on the

---

108 Jeffrey R. Holland, *Created for Greater Things* (Salt Lake City: Deseret Book, 2011).
109 Jeffrey R. Holland, "None Were with Him," *Ensign*, May 2009.

sea. They had waited for hours—even all through the night. Watching for Him to arrive on the shore, they desperately fought the waves, their hearts filled with dread. They were weary almost beyond their ability to endure, something you may have felt. When at last they saw Him walking across the water toward them, they did not recognize Him, and they cried out in fear.

Seeing their alarm, "Jesus spake unto them, saying, Be of good cheer; it is I; be not afraid" (Matthew 14:27). The second He recognized their trepidation, He spoke up to bring them comfort. He is not one who asks that you suffer needlessly. Ever.

And then Peter, that bold fisherman who so yearned to be like his Master, said, "Lord, if it be thou, bid me come unto thee on the water." And the Lord said simply, "Come" (Matthew 14:28–29).

With that unmistakable invitation from the Lord, Peter set out, walking on the water to Jesus. "But when he saw the wind boisterous, he was afraid; and beginning to sink, he cried, saying, Lord, save me. And immediately Jesus stretched forth his hand, and caught him, and said unto him, O thou of little faith, wherefore didst thou doubt?" (Matthew 14:30–31).

Of this powerful event, Elder David A. Bednar said, "I envision Peter responding fervently and immediately to the Savior's invitation. With his eyes fixed upon Jesus, he stepped out of the boat and miraculously walked on the water. Only when his gaze was diverted by the wind and the waves did he become afraid and begin to sink."[110]

You can likely identify with Peter. There, just a few arms' lengths away, was his Master—who had unmistakably invited Peter to come to Him over the stormy sea. Not *through* the waves, but *over* them. So Peter started out, defying all natural laws and heeding instead the laws of the One who rules the universe.

But then something heartbreaking—something wretchedly human—happened. Peter diverted his gaze from the Savior, the One who makes all things possible. Instead of focusing on Jesus Christ, Peter glanced down at the waters of the Galilee, waters that were being churned by the furious winds. His mind, once filled with the peace and possibility offered by the Savior, was now consumed by the sheer impossibility of what he was doing. And with that simple diversion, he began to sink.

For you, it is the same. Look to the Savior and feel the peace that only He can bring. Or look away—at all the distressing situations in your life,

110 David A. Bednar, "Therefore They Hushed Their Fears," *Ensign*, May 2015.

at all the chaos in the world, at the utter impossibility of making it through whatever is besieging you—and start to sink. Trust in your own inadequate abilities, or "Look unto me in every thought; doubt not, fear not" (D&C 6:36).

It is only by looking to Him, trusting in Him, that you can find everlasting peace. And it is solidly within your ability to do so. Elder Bednar counseled, "Correct knowledge of and faith in the Lord empower us to hush our fears because Jesus Christ is the only source of enduring peace. He declared, 'Learn of me, and listen to my words; walk in the meekness of my Spirit, and you shall have peace in me' (D&C 19:23)."[111]

Elder Holland likewise wrote, "In a world of some discouragement, sorrow, and overmuch sin, in times when fear and despair seem to prevail, when humanity is feverish with no worldly physicians in sight, I too say, 'Trust Jesus.' Let Him still the tempest and ride upon the storm."[112]

In your search for peace, don't forget one of the most essential elements of calm and tranquility: utilize the Savior's magnificent Atonement to rid yourself of the peace-robbing effects of sin in your life. Of this, Elder Holland said:

> I don't know what things may be troubling you personally, but, even knowing how terrific you are and how faithfully you are living, I would be surprised if someone somewhere weren't troubled by a transgression or the temptation of transgression. To you, wherever you may be, I say, Come unto Him and lay down your burden. Let Him lift the load. Let Him give peace to your soul. Nothing in this world is more burdensome than sin—it is the heaviest cross men and women ever bear.[113]

Sometimes the road to repentance can seem almost too difficult. It may seem a path so strewn with treacherous obstacles that it is beyond your ability to travel. Compared to the grueling, exhausting burden of sin—the "heaviest cross," as Elder Holland described it—the path to forgiveness can pale in

111 Ibid.
112 Jeffrey R. Holland, *Created for Greater Things* (Salt Lake City: Deseret Book, 2011).
113 Jeffrey R. Holland, "Come unto Me," *Ensign*, Apr. 1998; adapted from a Church Educational System young adult fireside given on March 2, 1997 at Brigham Young University.

comparison. He invites you to lay down your burden at His feet, to let His ever-merciful shoulders bear your liability. There is nothing random in that invitation. He *wants* to take that weight from you—to spare you the worry and despair that go along with it. He literally gave His life for your ability to do exactly that.

So if there are things for which you need to be forgiven, ask for His divine forgiveness. If there are things you need to confess, experience the soul-healing power of confession. If there are things you need to forget, let Him help you clear those things from your mind and heart. And if there are things you need to improve or change, enlist His help in building the soul you imagine and for which you yearn—for, after all, He is the master builder.[114]

When you come unto Him and experience the forgiveness made possible through His Atonement, you "shall dwell safely, and shall be quiet from fear of evil" (Proverbs 1:33). You will experience a deep, quenching, satisfying peace that comes in no other way. It comes in no other way because He *is* The Way.

In all the "solutions" the world may offer you, the sure solution is magnificent in its simplicity. It is Jesus Christ, He who promises that our hearts need not be troubled or afraid (see John 14:27), He who helps us hush our fears. Elder Bednar promises,

> Exercising faith in and on the holy name of Jesus Christ, meekly submitting to His will and timing in our lives, and humbly acknowledging His hand in all things yield the peaceable things of the kingdom of God that bring joy and eternal life (see D&C 42:61). Even as we encounter difficulties and face the uncertainties of the future, we can cheerfully persevere and live a "peaceable life in all godliness and honesty" (1 Timothy 2:2).[115]

He writhed in agony against all the evils and temptations and difficulties of this world for *you*. He gave His life on the cross and raised Himself again as He promised for *you*. Inherent in all that is the fact the he wants *you* to

---

114 See Jeffrey R. Holland, *Created for Greater Things* (Salt Lake City: Deseret Book, 2011).

115 David A. Bednar, "Therefore They Hushed Their Fears," *Ensign*, May 2015.

experience the peace He makes possible. He doesn't want you to struggle or cry or feel abandoned for one more minute. He wants to give you the peace He has already purchased and paid for.

Know you can have that peace now. It's not something you have to postpone—to look forward to only in the next life, after all the extremities of this life have been removed. The promise is yours, and you can redeem it right now.

Elder Holland said, "Christ and His angels and His prophets forever labor to buoy up our spirits, steady our nerves, calm our hearts, send us forth with renewed strength and resolute hope. . . . Christ has overcome the world (see John 16:33). Through His suffering and His obedience He has earned and rightly bears the crown of 'Prince of Peace.'"[116]

That is your promise as you turn to Him. As you stay focused on Him. As you refuse to divert your gaze to the storm-tossed sea that rages around you. "His power and peace are real."[117] They are the most real things you can rely on as you make your way back to heaven. Elder Holland was speaking of *you* when he said, "There certainly can and will be plenty of external difficulties in life; nevertheless, the soul that comes unto Christ dwells within a personal fortress, a veritable palace of perfect peace."[118]

116 Jeffrey R. Holland, "The Peaceable Things of the Kingdom," *Ensign*, Nov. 1996.
117 David A. Bednar, "Therefore They Hushed Their Fears," *Ensign*, May 2015
118 Jeffrey R. Holland, "Come unto Me," *Ensign*, Apr. 1998; adapted from a Church Educational System young adult fireside given on March 2, 1997, at Brigham Young University.

"THE BLESSINGS OF THE LORD
BE UPON YOU"
Believing in The Promise

> *"Just because God is God, just because Christ is Christ,*
> *they . . . can't help but bless us. They have to.*
> *It is their nature."*
> —Elder Jeffrey R. Holland[119]

BOTH SCRIPTURE AND MODERN-DAY REVELATION are bursting with the promises God makes to His faithful children. Among those are the ones made specifically to His daughters, for whom He holds such a tender spot in His heart.

Other promises have also been given. Every covenant—beginning with the very act of baptism—is a two-way promise that includes within its specific and exquisite language the promise of a blessing.

Perhaps without even realizing it, you are well exercised in covenants and promises. Every week, faithful Latter-day Saints—you among them— come from all walks of life and from every circumstance to sup at the Lord's table, to partake of the sacrament and thus renew those covenants made in the waters of baptism. You come each week, your spirit—and sometimes your body—battered and broken by the extremities of life. There, in communion with your fellow-citizens in the kingdom, you bow your head and offer up your broken heart, your contrite spirit—your desire to do better, to be better. And in that singular ordinance you are offered the

---

119 Jeffrey R. Holland, "Come unto Me," *Ensign*, Apr. 1998; adapted from a Church Educational System young adult fireside given on March 2, 1997, at Brigham Young University.

merciful chance to *be* better—with a sure promise that after all you can do, He will make up the difference. That is His promise to you, and a blessing He gives freely.

In addition to all of that language of promise, you also have promises directly from Heavenly Father to you. They are yours alone. His promises meant just for you flowed through a patriarch who laid his hands on your head and revealed to you the paths you could follow and the blessings you would receive based on your faithfulness and obedience. Armed with that blessing, you have not only a divine blueprint but a sweet description of the things your Father has in store for you.

So what if you have waited patiently, exercising faith and obedience, and promised blessings have not come?

What then?

How long can you continue to hope and pray and wait? How long must you continue to approach your Heavenly Father and His Son, Jesus Christ, kneeling at their throne of grace and pleading in meekness and lowliness of heart for fulfillment of promises already given?

When can you expect promises to be fulfilled?

There is no precise answer to that. No one but God Himself knows when promises to you will be fulfilled. But you can be certain of one thing: Heavenly Father *never* breaks His promises. He never has, and He never will. And so you have this surety: if you have a promise, you can also be certain that it will be fulfilled.

It can be extremely difficult, even painful, to wait for a promise that has not yet been fulfilled. It's easy to wonder whether the promise has been forgotten—whether a God who has charge of the entire universe might have become so involved with something much more global in nature that He has—for the time, anyway—failed to remember His promise to you. After all, there are wars ripping apart nations and crowded camps housing desperate refugees and governments on the brink of collapsing, not to mention an ongoing battle against evil. Any of those and thousands of things like them must consume His time and energy. While the longed-for promise may consume *your* every thought, you reason, it just may pale in comparison to all those other matters flooding into the eyes and ears and mind of your Heavenly Father.

But that's not how it works. With our very mortal and finite minds, we can't even begin to comprehend how He keeps track of it all and manages to grant it all—but we can be assured that He does. The promises He has made to you are every bit as visible on His radar screen as is any threat or disaster or political upheaval. They are also every bit as visible on His radar screen as the promises He has made to every one of His children; no one takes a back seat.

It may be grueling to come to terms with a promise yet unfulfilled, but that doesn't mean you should give up—that you should decide, after a time that seems too drawn out, that the promise will *not* be delivered. Because here is another promise—one from an Apostle of God, a special witness appointed to represent Him:

> Don't you quit. You keep walking. You keep trying. There is help and happiness ahead. . . . It will be all right in the end. Trust God and believe in good things to come. . . . Some blessings come soon, some come late, and some don't come until heaven; but for those who embrace the gospel of Jesus Christ, *they come.*[120]

There you have it—a promise you can depend on: *Some blessings come soon. Some come late. Some don't come until heaven. It will be all right in the end.*

Right now, as you try to patiently wait for a promised blessing that seems to occupy your every thought, it might be hard to imagine that the blessing *will* arrive at all. If you find yourself in that situation, remember that sometimes we see blessings granted and promises fulfilled only through the powerful lens of hindsight. It is only through looking back that we recognize them for what they are.

President Dieter F. Uchtdorf counseled, "Often the deep valleys of our present will be understood only by looking back on them from the mountains of our future experience. Often we can't see the Lord's hand in our lives until long after trials have passed. Often the most difficult times of our lives are essential building blocks that form the foundation of our character and pave the way to future opportunity, understanding, and happiness."[121]

As you wait, don't fall into the trap of fearing that there simply may not be enough—that you are potentially waiting for blessings that may

---

120 Jeffrey R. Holland, "An High Priest of Good Things to Come," *Ensign*, Nov. 1999.
121 Dieter F. Uchtdorf, "Continue in Patience," *Ensign*, May 2010.

not come because God is running out of them. *Abundance*—overflowing, a quantity more than sufficient—applies here. Looking through the lens of abundance with our Heavenly Father's help, we are assured that "there is no end to the blessings available to His children."[122]

CES educator David A. Christensen writes, "Heavenly Father wants to give us blessings, assurances of His love, and help along our way. After all, His whole purpose and glory is to give us all that He has. If He gives us all that He has, then we could interpret that He won't have anything left for Himself. Not so, not even close. His blessing and abundance is plenty and enough for all."[123]

The Lord Himself tells us, "For the earth is full, and there is enough and to spare" (D&C 104:17). No one will go away empty-handed. Not even you.

Consider this: the time while you are waiting for a promised blessing to be fulfilled might be a gift from the Lord—an opportunity to learn and grow and discover the ways of God. That might be a searing thought while you are in the midst of waiting. But think of the Prophet Joseph Smith languishing in Liberty Jail, the most squalid environment imaginable. Day by day he and his companions were subjected not only to imprisonment but to freezing temperatures, filthy conditions, contaminated food, and abuse. His confinement there went on, day after dreary day, for more than five months.

While incarcerated, he learned through letters of the depravities to which his people were being subjected. Driven to the extremity of his own endurance, he poured out his heart in an impassioned plea to the Lord, undoubtedly wondering about the blessings he and they had been promised. Crying with all the intensity of his heart, he asked:

> O God, where art thou? . . .
>
> How long shall thy hand be stayed, and thine eye, yea thy pure eye, behold from the eternal heavens the wrongs of thy people and of thy servants, and thine ear be penetrated with their cries?
>
> Yea, O Lord, how long shall they suffer these wrongs and unlawful oppressions, before thine heart shall be softened toward them, and thy bowels be moved with compassion toward them? (D&C 121:1–3)

---

122 David A. Christensen, *A Thankful Heart: 31 Teachings to Recognize Blessings in Your Life* (Springville: Cedar Fort, 2015).
123 Ibid.

In response, Joseph received one of the most poignant revelations ever recorded—one that speaks to us today as we struggle with the trials we suffer as we wait for the promised blessings. Speaking of the yet-unfulfilled blessings in store for His Saints, the Lord said, "[K]now thou, my son, that all these things shall give thee experience, and shall be for thy good. The Son of Man hath descended below them all. Art thou greater than he?" (D&C 122:7–8).

In that divine answer, we receive so much. First, we know where to go for succor: to the Lord, who descended below every pain imaginable in the terrible arithmetic of Gethsemane so He would know how to best comfort and sustain us in our trials. Second, we are taught that the expanse of time while we wait for blessings to come can be a time for gaining valued experience that might not come in any other way. We may, while living through those extremities, gain the strength and experience to endure even greater trials that come later. We may also find the ability to spiritually and mentally come to sublime understanding.

It was the Prophet Joseph, who so paved the way for us, who said, "The things of God are of deep import; and time, and experience, and careful and ponderous and solemn thoughts can only find them out."[124]

While you wait for blessings to come, your time and thoughts and experience may yet prepare you for greater blessings.

A wonderful example of that principle was related by General Authority Emeritus John H. Groberg.[125] One day a faithful couple came to his office in search of a blessing. They had tried for several years to conceive a child without success, despite countless hours spent with doctors and in prayer. While this sweet and faithful woman had already received many priesthood blessings, she and her husband asked if Elder Groberg would be willing to assist in giving her another. He felt impressed to do so.

As Elder Groberg was delivering the blessing and pleading for heaven's inspiration, he received a strong impression. Following that direction, he promised the wife that she would bear a child. The couple left his office imbued with a renewed sense of hope, crowned with a blessing and the promise for which they had so yearned.

A year or so later, the same couple again visited Elder Groberg. He wrote, "They had that same wonderful spirit of love and faith about them. I remembered the impression I had to promise that she would bear a child, so

124 *History of the Church*, vol. 3, 295.
125 Story adapted from John H. Groberg, *Eternity Is Now* (American Fork: Covenant Communications, 2016), 33–36.

I was a little surprised when they not only came without a child, but she was not pregnant."126

This committed woman then related a story that was at once inspiring and heartbreaking. A few months after receiving the blessing from Elder Groberg, she was elated to learn that she was pregnant. Her joy was indescribable. Every day she prayed, thanking God for this incredible blessing in her life. From the moment she learned she was expecting, she loved her baby with a powerful devotion; she could not wait for the opportunity to raise and teach and train this long-awaited child.

Her pregnancy went smoothly until about two weeks before her due date. One day she could feel that something was not right. She was rushed to the hospital, where a fully formed, beautiful baby girl was delivered. The precious infant took two or three small gasps of air and then was gone.

You can scarcely imagine the pain and sorrow and frustration this devoted woman felt. She mourned for weeks. Feeling broken and driven to her knees, she repeatedly sought the Lord in prayer, thorny questions streaming through her mind. *What happened? And why did it happen? What about those years of waiting and months of patient preparation? And what about the blessing I received—what happened to my promise?*

Maybe you can see her there, on her knees, sending her strangled prayers heavenward through her tears and despair. Maybe you have had a similar experience. Her spirit felt torn, bouncing between the heartache of loss and the feeling of love for and trust in the Lord. Then one day as she was expressing her grief to Him, wrote Elder Groberg, "a new light flooded over her that washed away any doubt, guilt, or frustration she might have had."127

Describing that light, she said to Elder Groberg, "You remember the promise from the Lord you gave me? It was that I would 'bear' a child, not that I would 'raise' one. I bore a daughter. She is mine; she is ours. His promise is fulfilled. I should not complain. Those months of preparation should not be wasted with questioning or doubt. They will become a bulwark of faith and love that my husband and I can build on for all eternity. It has taken time and effort to understand this, but I am deeply grateful for Him and the increased faith and love He has given me."128

As Elder Groberg looked at this couple, holding hands and calmly sharing their faith and love, he could not hold back his tears. After they

126 Groberg, 33–34.
127 Groberg, 34.
128 Ibid.

left, he began to see in a new light many difficult things that he and others had been through. As he rehearsed those things in his mind, he knew that "throughout all of eternity, faithfulness will be rewarded and every promised blessing will be received by the faithful."[129]

The couple with whom Elder Groberg visited were not able to have any more biological children. However, they were eventually able to adopt children and raise their family in righteousness. For them, the blessings did come. Joseph Smith said, "You will have the joy, the pleasure, and satisfaction of nurturing this child, after its resurrection, until it reaches the full stature of its spirit."[130] As Elder Holland promised, it was "all right in the end."[131] And as President Uchtdorf predicted, this couple—and others like them—were able to understand their deep valleys "only by looking back on them from the mountains of [their] future experience."[132]

As you think of this woman, one who had suffered unimaginable heartbreak at the loss of her baby, remember what she said: "We must not waste this preparation time." Whenever you wait for promised blessings to arrive, whenever you find that waiting to be a sorely difficult time that tries your faith, remember that the waiting presents a singular opportunity to meditate, to pray, to praise, and to acknowledge the hand of God in your life and in all things. Such time gives you a unique opportunity to figure out the ways and will of a loving God.

If you are still waiting for a promised blessing to come, take hope in the promise of Elder M. Russell Ballard: "Through your faith and personal righteousness in keeping the commandments of the Lord Jesus Christ, you can qualify for all of the blessings our Heavenly Father has promised to His obedient children. Some of you may not have an opportunity in mortality to fulfill every righteous desire of your heart. *But you can be certain that no eternal blessing will be denied you* if you remain faithful and live the principles of the gospel throughout your earthly life."[133]

No eternal blessing will be denied you. That promise comes to you from an Apostle, another special witness of Jesus Christ—One we know will never, ever break His promises.

---

129 Groberg, 35.
130 Teachings of Presidents of the Church: Joseph F. Smith (Salt Lake City: The Church of Jesus Christ of Latter-day Saints, 2011), 128–35.
131 Jeffrey R. Holland, "An High Priest of Good Things to Come," *Ensign*, Nov. 1999.
132 Dieter F. Uchtdorf, "Continue in Patience," *Ensign*, May 2010.
133 M. Russell Ballard, "Be an Example of the Believers," *Ensign*, Nov. 1991; emphasis added.

As women, the promised blessings most tender to us are those concerning marriage and the opportunity to have children. Our hearts are centered on our potential roles as wives and mothers, and when those blessings seem to pass us by, they can bring considerable heartache. We go to our knees and to our secret places wondering where those blessings are—and, if driven by enough despair, wondering where the God is who purports to hear our prayers.

In these matters too we have visionary statements from prophets and Apostles. President James E. Faust assured us, "The prophets of the Lord have repeatedly promised that no blessing will be denied to the righteous single sisters of the Church if, through no fault of their own, they have not been married in this life and sealed to a worthy priesthood holder. They will be able to enjoy that blessing forever in the next world."[134]

And President Boyd K. Packer promised:

> Those who do not marry or those who cannot have children are not excluded from the eternal blessings they seek but which, for now, remain beyond their reach. We do not always know how or when blessings will present themselves, but the promise of eternal increase will not be denied any faithful individual who makes and keeps sacred covenants.
>
> Your secret yearnings and tearful pleadings will touch the heart of both the Father and the Son. You will be given a personal assurance from Them that your life will be full and that no blessing that is essential will be lost to you.
>
> As a servant of the Lord, acting in the office to which I have been ordained, I give those in such circumstances a promise that there will be nothing essential to your salvation and exaltation that shall not in due time rest upon you. Arms now empty will be filled, and hearts now hurting from broken dreams and yearning will be healed.[135]

Arms now empty will be filled. Hearts now hurting will be healed. Those promised blessings are yours. You can clasp them tight to your heart against the day they will be fulfilled—and they will be fulfilled. For, as President Spencer W. Kimball promised, "[P]lease know that our Father in

134 James E. Faust, "You Are All Heaven Sent," *Ensign*, Nov. 2002.
135 Boyd K. Packer, "The Witness," *Ensign*, May 2014.

Heaven is aware of your anguish, and that one day he will bless you beyond your capacity to express."[136]

While we are in the middle of that anguish, "we can get sucked into feeling that heaven has withdrawn and the Lord has abandoned us. During these times, it is unfortunately easy to focus on our challenges and deprivations. We get discouraged, lose hope for better days, and feel like our uncomfortable station in life is permanent. We forget to count our blessings, we lose our awareness of His hand in our lives, and we get depressed."[137]

So while you are waiting—while you are anticipating a promised blessing, no matter what it is—watch. Observe. Look for the blessings you are receiving, because they are there. Even while you wait for one particular blessing, one meaningful promise for which you yearn, don't overlook all the blessings that are being poured out upon you, day after day, by a Father who loves you and wants to remind you of His care. Elder Jeffrey R. Holland counsels:

> If we constantly focus only on the stones in our mortal path, we will almost surely miss the beautiful flower or cool stream provided by the loving Father who outlined our journey. Each day can bring more joy than sorrow when our mortal and spiritual eyes are open to God's goodness. Joy in the gospel is not something that begins only in the next life. It is our privilege now, this very day. We must never allow our burdens to obscure our blessings. *There will always be more blessings than burdens*—even if some days it doesn't seem so. . . . Enjoy those blessings right now. They are yours and always will be.[138]

So look for those blessings—the ones that *do* come. They will come even (and maybe especially) in the times when your life may be at its most challenging—at the end of your fourth watch. Sometimes they will seem so insignificant that you might miss them unless you are focused. And

136 Spencer W. Kimball, "The Role of Righteous Women," *Ensign*, Nov. 1979, 103.
137 David A. Christensen, *A Thankful Heart: 31 Teachings to Recognize Blessings in Your Life* (Springville: Cedar Fort, 2015).
138 Jeffrey R. Holland, "What I Wish Every New Member Knew—and Every Longtime Member Remembered," *Ensign*, Nov. 2006; emphasis added.

remember that no blessing from God is *ever* insignificant, no matter how small. Every day, ask yourself how God blessed you that day. President Henry B. Eyring promised that if "you do that long enough and with faith, you will find yourself remembering blessings. And sometimes, you will have gifts brought to your mind which you failed to notice during the day, but which you will then know were a touch of God's hand in your life."[139]

In your quest to recognize the blessings poured out upon you while you wait for one yet to come, don't overlook the power of gratitude. President Thomas S. Monson asked, "Do we remember to give thanks for the blessings we receive? Sincerely giving thanks not only *helps us recognize our blessings*, but it also unlocks the doors of heaven and helps us feel God's love."[140]

What a powerful equation: instead of feeling abandoned by heaven, you can feel unequaled love and abiding care from the other side of the veil. You can gain the warm assurance that your Father in Heaven is aware of you and is preparing to pour out the blessings you have been promised.

Remember the woman of faith who anonymously, and probably with great embarrassment, pushed her way through the crowds for the chance to simply touch the hem of the Savior's robe, knowing it would heal her (see Matthew 9:20)? She had suffered for *twelve years* from an issue of blood, being ostracized and shut out from the society she had known. Desperate to be healed, "she said within herself, If I may but touch his garment, I shall be whole. But Jesus turned him about, and when he saw her, he said, Daughter, be of good comfort; thy faith hath made thee whole. And the woman was made whole from that hour" (Matthew 9:21–22).

The Savior has invited you, "Come, follow me" (Luke 18:22). His is not a vain invitation or a random supplication; He asks you to follow Him because He knows the sure way to happiness, the certain way to the place where you can realize fulfillment of the blessings He has promised you. When He issues that invitation, He "means that he knows where the quicksand is and where the thorns are and the best way to handle the slippery slope near the summit of our personal mountains. He knows it all, and he knows the way. He is the way."[141]

---

139 Henry B. Eyring, "Remembrance and Gratitude," *Ensign*, Nov. 1989.
140 Thomas S. Monson, "The Divine Gift of Gratitude," *Ensign*, Nov. 2010; emphasis added.
141 Jeffrey R. Holland, "Come Unto Me," *Ensign*, Apr. 1998.

If you have not yet developed the faith of the woman who pressed through the crowd to touch the hem of the Savior's garment, borrow her faith. Borrow hers until yours is strong enough. Rely on her knowledge that if you can but follow the way of the Savior, you can be healed—can be assured "that the promised blessing will come, that the promise is true because it comes from God."[142]

---

142 Henry B. Eyring, *Because He First Loved Us* (Salt Lake City: Deseret Book, 2002).

"GOD HATH NOT GIVEN US
THE SPIRIT OF FEAR"

Facing Life When You Are Afraid

*"You need never be discouraged or afraid. The way through
difficulties has always been prepared for you, and
you will find it if you exercise faith."*
—President Henry B. Eyring[143]

IT WAS 1933 WHEN PRESIDENT Franklin D. Roosevelt delivered his first inaugural address. A quarter of the nation was unemployed, many could not feed their families, and the world teetered between two catastrophic world wars. In his address, the president tried with all his capacity to calm legions of frightened Americans with his now-famous creed: "The only thing we have to fear is fear itself."[144]

His insight was timeless. And even though his address was given more than eighty years ago, there is no expiration date on fear; it simply parades itself in new, updated clothing with every passing year.

There is no way Roosevelt could have envisioned the face of his country and the world more than eight decades after he challenged us to gain control of our fear. Today, we are living in the season predicted by the Lord: "And in that day . . . the whole earth shall be in commotion, and men's hearts shall fail them" (D&C 45:26). Globally, governments—even our own, some might argue—are unstable. Bloody civil wars send terrified refugees fleeing for their lives in search of a better and safer place where they can raise their children. Tent cities spring up, and mothers scratch for food to feed their families. Ethnic cleansing perpetrated by the most evil wipes out entire civilizations.

---

143 Henry B. Eyring, "Walk in the Light," *Ensign*, May 2008.
144 Franklin D. Roosevelt, First Inaugural Address, March 4, 1933.

Threats of nuclear weapon development cause us to view foreign powers with suspicion. Elementary school children have drills to prepare them for shooters in their hallways. The menace of terrorism victimizes innocent bystanders on the streets, at carnivals, in market places. Suicide bombers zero in on identified targets, not caring who else gets swept away in the carnage. Add to that countless threats of natural disaster, the increase in crime, the disease of pornography, and sexual predators lurking in the dark corners of social media.

These and other conditions breed fear. Even when geographically distant from such catastrophic events, it is common for us to be seized with alarm. The very *improbable*—that you will find yourself living in a refugee camp, unable to feed your children—somehow becomes the very *possible*: that you might lose your home when unemployment strikes or when a tornado sweeps through town. That *you* will be the one doling out the last loaf of bread as you count out food stamps in the wake of job loss. That *your* child will be taken down by a predator.

Fear is not a new emotion. As long ago as the Savior's visit to the people in Bountiful, He commanded them—and us—to "fear not" (3 Nephi 22:4). What's unique about fear in our day, the experts say, "is how people experience it. Since the 1980s, society at large has bolted frantically from one panic to the next. Fear of crime reduced us to wrecks, but before long we were also howling about deadly diseases, drug abusers, online pedophiles, avian flu, teens gone wild, mad cows, anthrax, immigrants, environmental collapse, and—let us not forget—terrorists."[145]

Fear is, teaches Elder David A. Bednar, a "potent emotion" that is "an important element of our mortal existence."[146] As an "important element" of our mortal existence, we know there will always be fear—the sudden, acute panic we feel in response to an unexpected threat (you know, the impossibly huge wolf spider that skitters out from behind the pile of firewood). That kind of fear will never go away. It is the global, overwhelming fear almost of life itself that is unnecessary. That's the kind of fear we're talking about here—the kind of fear that needs to and should be overcome.

One of the biggest problems with that kind of fear is that it incapacitates us, creates of us victims. And now experts tell us that for the first time in

145 Julie Hanus, "Overcoming Fear Culture and Fear Itself," *Utne Reader*, January–February 2009.
146 David A. Bednar, "Therefore They Hushed Their Fears," *Ensign*, May 2015.

history, fear is tearing our society apart. "The dangers of modern life have a stranglehold on people's imaginations. . . . [And] there's more at work here than frazzled modern nerves: Americans are fearful. Truly fearful. When they're asked, a majority say with certainty that the world is more dangerous than ever before. Even in the face of evidence that negates this misperception, there is no relief. We lock our doors, say our prayers, and still can't get to sleep."[147]

As we are grabbed more powerfully by fear of all kinds, "media outlets, politicians, and businesses all have learned to capitalize on this distinctly modern sense of dread, and thus profit from finding ways to cultivate it. Until we find a way to resist fear, we'll . . . be party to the personal, cultural, and political consequences."[148]

The consequences are dire. And on its surface, that task—to resist fear—may seem almost insurmountable. All you have to do is turn on a TV, listen to a radio, read a newspaper, or stand in the grocery checkout line scanning the headline stories on magazine covers. Society has become "increasingly sophisticated at communicating messages and information that produce fear responses. Advertising, political campaigns, news coverage, and social media all send the constant message that people should be afraid—*very* afraid."[149]

It's no wonder that many people feel afraid. There are clearly plenty of things to be afraid of. And in addition to global and national factors, there are also very private, individual matters that can rob us of peace and combine to generate fear.

If you feel afraid—of life and of your future—you know how devastating fear can be. It can make you feel isolated. Alone. Helpless. And when you get pulled into that cycle, it is difficult to gain enough perspective to believe that anything might help.

But there *is* help, regardless of what makes you afraid. And that help comes from the same source as all other help you are given: a loving Heavenly Father who watches over you and protects you. He promises you: "Fear thou not; for I am with thee: be not dismayed; for I am thy God: I will strengthen thee; yea, I

147 Julie Hanus, "Overcoming Fear Culture and Fear Itself," *Utne Reader*, January–February 2009.
148 Ibid.
149 Don Hazen, "Fear Dominates Politics, Media and Human Existence in America—And It's Getting Worse," *AlterNet*, March 1, 2015, http://www.alternet.org/fear-america/fear-dominates-politics-media-and-human-existence-america-and-its-getting-worse.

will help thee; yea, I will uphold thee with the right hand of my righteousness" (Isaiah 41:10).

Notice that God does not promise to take away your fear or the source of your fear. Instead, He promises to help you and strengthen you against the fear—to uphold you with His righteousness. With His help and strength, you are then able to conquer your fear.

A good example of exactly how this works occurred in the Book of Mormon when Alma's people were frightened by an advancing Lamanite army that seemed much larger and more powerful than they. Alma stood among his people "and exhorted them that they should not be frightened, but . . . should remember the Lord their God and he would deliver them. Therefore, they hushed their fears" (Mosiah 23:27–28).

"Notice Alma did not hush the people's fears," says Elder Bednar. "Rather, Alma counseled the believers to remember the Lord and the deliverance only He could bestow (see 2 Nephi 2:8). And *knowledge of the Savior's protecting watchcare enabled the people to hush their own fears.* Correct knowledge of and faith in the Lord empower us to hush our fears because Jesus Christ is the only source of enduring peace."[150]

He is the source of enduring peace because He "allows us to view mortality through the precious perspective of eternity" and because He "helps us maintain a consistent focus on our heavenly destination. Thus, we can be blessed to hush our fears because His doctrine provides purpose and direction in all aspects of our lives. His ordinances and covenants fortify and comfort in times both good and bad. And His priesthood authority gives assurance that the things that matter most can endure both in time and in eternity."[151]

He has not only the capacity but the desire to strengthen you, help you, and uphold you, a priceless knowledge that can be the first step to overcoming fear of any kind. It is that faith that can calm your heart and ease your fear, regardless of the demons that can make you afraid.

You are not alone; all of us have those demons. But all of us also have access to the divine help that can transform any fear. Elder Neil L. Andersen teaches, "Challenges, difficulties, questions, doubts—these are part of our mortality. But we are not alone. As disciples of the Lord Jesus

---

150 David A. Bednar, "Therefore They Hushed Their Fears," *Ensign*, May 2015; emphasis added.
151 Ibid.

Christ, we have enormous spiritual reservoirs of light and truth available to us. Fear and faith cannot coexist in our hearts at the same time. In our days of difficulty, we choose the road of faith. Jesus said, 'Be not afraid, only believe' (Mark 5:36)."[152]

There it is, directly from the mouth of an Apostle: fear and faith cannot coexist. And there it is, directly from the Lord Himself: an invitation to believe instead of being afraid. In Him is the great balm—"For God hath not given us the spirit of fear; but of power, and of love, and of a sound mind" (2 Timothy 1:7).

Elder Kevin W. Pearson of the Seventy echoed that same truth when he said, "Faith and fear cannot coexist. One gives way to the other. The simple fact is we all need to constantly build faith and overcome sources of destructive disbelief. . . . We do have a choice. We get what we focus on consistently. Because there is an opposition in all things, there are forces that erode our faith." As we grapple with doubts, those things that can erode our faith, Elder Pearson teaches that doubt "does not come from the Light of Christ or the influence of the Holy Ghost. Doubt is a negative emotion related to fear. . . . It is inconsistent with our divine identity as children of God."[153]

The Lord has invited you, "Look unto me in every thought; doubt not, fear not" (D&C 6:36). He pleads with you to give the lion's share of your thoughts to Him with the greatest amount of faith you can muster—and promises that fear cannot fill your heart and mind if your heart and mind have already been given over to Him in faith.

"Faith is a spiritual gift from God that comes through the Holy Ghost," Elder Pearson counsels. "There is no other thing in which we can have absolute assurance. There is no other foundation in life that can bring the same peace, joy, and hope. In uncertain and difficult times, faith is truly a spiritual gift worthy of our utmost efforts."[154]

If ever a man had cause to be filled with fear, it was Elisha. Preparing to fight for Israel against its much more powerful enemy, Syria, Elisha and his servants woke one morning to learn that the entire city of Dothan was surrounded by the enemy's ferocious troops. When a trembling servant asked what they were to do, Elisha responded, "Fear not: for they that

152 Neil L. Anderson, "You Know Enough," *Ensign*, Nov. 2008.
153 Kevin W. Pearson, "Faith in the Lord Jesus Christ," *Ensign*, May 2009.
154 Ibid.

be with us are more than they that be with them" (2 Kings 6:16). Elisha then prayed that the young man's eyes would be opened—"And the Lord opened the eyes of the young man; and he saw: and, behold, the mountain was full of horses and chariots of fire round about Elisha" (2 Kings 6:17).

You can count on that same thing: *those that be with you are greater and more powerful than they that be with anything you fear.* Elder Jeffrey R. Holland promised, "In the gospel of Jesus Christ you have help from both sides of the veil, and you must never forget that. When disappointment and discouragement strike—and they will—you remember and *never forget* that if our eyes could be opened we would see horses and chariots of fire as far as the eye can see riding at reckless speed to come to our protection. They will always be there, these armies of heaven, in defense of Abraham's seed."[155]

That is your promise—armies as far as the eye can see, *riding at reckless speed to come to your protection.* And you have an even greater promise as you exercise faith in the Lord Jesus Christ: "Behold, this is the promise of the Lord unto you. . . . Wherefore, be of good cheer, and do not fear, for I the Lord am with you, and will stand by you; and ye shall bear record of me, even Jesus Christ, that I am the Son of the living God, that I was, that I am, and that I am to come" (D&C 68:5–6).

He will be with you. He will stand by you. And because of that, you need not fear. Elder Quentin L. Cook reaffirmed that promise when he said, "It is our faith in Jesus Christ that sustains us at the crossroads of life's journey. It is the first principle of the gospel. Without it we will spin our wheels at the intersection, spending our precious time but getting nowhere. It is Christ who offers the invitation to follow Him, to give Him our burden. . . ."[156]

It was the Psalmist who penned, "The Lord is my light and my salvation; whom shall I fear? the Lord is the strength of my life; of whom shall I be afraid?" (Psalms 27:1). This simple verse provides the formula for conquering fear: exercising faith in the Lord, who is your strength. Faith is exactly that powerful. Fear, on the other hand, says Bongani Nyathi, "is the devil's poison to disturb you from having a close relationship with God."

As you develop that close relationship with God and work on building your faith, there may be moments when fear still impacts you. At those moments, envision the armies who surround you and wait to ride with reckless

---

155 Jeffrey R. Holland, *Created for Greater Things* (Salt Lake City: Deseret Book, 2011); emphasis added.
156 Quentin L. Cook, "Live By Faith and Not By Fear," *Ensign*, Nov. 2007.

speed to come to your protection. And then move forward, investing your faith in those armies. General Norman Schwarzkopf, former Commander-in-chief of the United States Central Command, who led all the coalition forces in the Gulf War, said, "True courage is being afraid, and going ahead and doing your job anyhow."

Even if there is still a vestige of fear, know that your boldest efforts will prevail. Know that your reliance on the Lord will get you through. Even in the face of failure, you can be certain that the Lord will be there to uphold you in your righteous efforts. Allen Neuharth, founder of *USA Today* and one of the most influential figures in the publishing industry, said, "I quit being afraid when my first venture failed and the sky didn't fall down." Feel confident in your knowledge that the Lord will never let your sky fall down.

As you go on—as you move ahead despite your lingering fear, your heart filled with faith that your fear will be conquered, you will find the courage that will quiet all your concerns. Author Toni Sorenson wrote, "So what if you're scared spitless? So what if you're intimidated, insecure, or inundated with doubt? If it's the thing that will advance you, do it anyway. Forward movement always begins with an inner decision."

Moving toward faith is always the antidote to fear. It is always the best inner decision.

What if your fear is not of outside forces—possible nuclear war, school shootings, economic disaster—but of your own weakness? Can your faith in God overcome *that* fear?

Absolutely.

The Lord has promised, "And if men come unto me I will show unto them their weakness. I give unto men weakness that they may be humble; and my grace is sufficient for all men that humble themselves before me; for if they humble themselves before me, and have faith in me, then will I make weak things become strong unto them" (Ether 12:27). His is the great healing power that will take away whatever is making you afraid—whether it is in the arena of war or the shadows of your own heart and soul.

It is to Him that you should look for help in this entire effort, for it is He who has the answers and who knows best how to succor and help you. Never forget that. The answer lies not in earthly but heavenly assistance. For, as C. S. Lewis so aptly wrote, "To what will you look for help if you will not look to that which is stronger than yourself?"[157]

---

157 C. S. Lewis, *Mere Christianity* (New York: HarperCollins, 1952).

Even with divine help, the process of turning your weaknesses into strengths is not one that happens overnight. It is one that takes careful tutoring and precise work on both the Father's part and on yours. But it *will* happen if you keep trying and keep exercising faith. President Dieter F. Uchtdorf says, "God wants to help us to eventually turn all of our weaknesses into strengths, but He knows that this is a long-term goal. He wants us to become perfect, and if we stay on the path of discipleship, one day we will. It's OK that you're not quite there yet. Keep working on it, but stop punishing yourself."[158]

We know that fear flourishes in weakness while faith thrives in strength. As you work to increase your own strength and banish your fear, be patient with yourself. Take things one step at a time. Elder David A. Bednar wrote, "If today you are a little bit better than you were yesterday, then that's enough. And, if tomorrow you are a little bit better than you were today, then that's enough."[159]

Whatever you do, don't give up on the process that can banish all your fears and bring you the quiet assurance of faith. Elder Holland challenges, "Stay in the race. Keep running. Keep walking. Keep praying. The Lord will renew your strength."[160]

Nephi provided the perfect formula for you as you work for the strength that will help you hush your fears: "Wherefore, ye must press forward with a steadfastness in Christ, having a perfect brightness of hope, and a love of God and of all men. Wherefore, if ye shall press forward, feasting upon the word of Christ, and endure to the end, behold, thus saith the Father: Ye shall have eternal life" (2 Nephi 31:20).

Referring to Nephi's divine instruction, Elder Bednar says:

> The disciplined endurance described in this verse is the result of spiritual understanding and vision, persistence, patience, and God's grace. Exercising faith in and on the holy name of Jesus Christ, meekly submitting to His will and timing in our lives, and humbly acknowledging His hand in all things yield the peaceable things of the kingdom of God

158 Dieter F. Uchtdorf, "Forget Me Not," *Ensign*, Nov. 2011.
159 David A. Bednar, *Act in Doctrine: Spiritual Patterns for Turning from Self to the Savior* (Salt Lake City: Deseret Book, 2012).
160 Jeffrey R. Holland, *For Times of Trouble: Spiritual Solace from the Psalms* (Salt Lake City: Deseret Book, 2012).

that bring joy and eternal life (see D&C 42:61). Even as we encounter difficulties and face the uncertainties of the future, we can cheerfully persevere and live a "peaceable life in all godliness and honesty" (1 Timothy 2:2).

We can be blessed to hush our fears as we receive the fortitude that comes from learning and living gospel principles and resolutely pressing forward on the covenant pathway.[161]

The Lord is ever watching over you. He knows what you need. He is kind, He loves you, and He will provide all things for your good—even a way to help you conquer fear. You no longer need to be afraid; in addition to helping you hush your own fears, President Uchtdorf promised, "There are times when we have to step into the darkness in faith"—and when we do, we can be "confident that God will place solid ground beneath our feet."[162]

---

161 David A. Bednar, "Therefore They Hushed Their Fears," *Ensign*, May 2015.
162 Dieter F. Uchtdorf, "Move Forward in Faith," *Ensign*, Aug. 2013.

YOU CAN LOVE

Being an Instrument in His Hands

*"With the help of the Holy Ghost, we can create an
emotionally healing place for the discriminated against,
the rejected, and the stranger. In these tender yet powerful ways,
we build the kingdom of God. Sisters, all of us came to earth with
these life-giving, nurturing, maternal gifts
because that is God's plan."*
—Neill F. Marriott[163]

THE DAY BEFORE I WAS scheduled to begin writing this chapter, I almost died.

Literally.

I will spare the more difficult details, but I was delivering a presentation to a youth group on how to spiritually prepare for a mission when I suffered a heart attack and a stroke. When I arrived at the emergency room, I was minutes from a coma. Over the ensuing weeks, the world-class cardiac surgeon who performed a quadruple bypass on my wounded heart repeatedly told me there was no medical reason I survived.

There may not have been a medical reason, but there was a divine reason (and I am still discovering what that reason is). What happened during the ensuing six weeks brought me closer to the love of my Heavenly Father and Savior—as well as the love of angels in mortality who created an emotionally healing place—than I have ever been.

I'm not sure I will ever approach anything quite like it again.

And it has provided a unique and singular perspective for this final chapter.

Because of my complicated medical condition, I had to stay in the hospital for eleven days before the surgery could be performed on my heart.

163 Neill F. Marriott, "What Shall We Do?" *Ensign*, May 2016.

Right away, that very first day, I experienced what Elder Jeffrey R. Holland spoke of when he wrote, "Someone you know is carrying a spiritual or physical or emotional burden of some sort, or some other affliction drawn from life's catalog of a thousand kinds of sorrow." He issued a challenge to all of us: "In the spirit of Christ's first invitation to His Apostles, jump into this work. Help people. Heal old wounds and try to make things better."[164]

That very first day, and for so many days afterward, I was surrounded by those who were trying to make things better. They were the angels our Father and Savior intended them to be. They had become powerful instruments in the hand of God, bringing His love and blessings directly to me.

When we "speak of those who are instruments in the hand of God," Elder Holland says, "we are reminded that not all angels are from the other side of the veil. Some of them we walk with and talk with—here, now, every day. . . . Indeed heaven never seems closer than when we see the love of God manifested in the kindness and devotion of people so good and so pure that angelic is the only word that comes to mind."[165]

During this life-altering time, I experienced the angelic acts of those I walked and talked with. There were meals and gifts and floral arrangements that filled my room with the beauty of God's creations. There were visits that brought words of encouragement and love on their wings. There were cards and letters and smiles. One woman sat at the foot of my chair and, using a sweetly perfumed lotion, rubbed my aching feet while she soothed my soul with her words of cheer and reassurance. Still another, knowing my diet was severely restricted, arrived with a basket of sugar-free candies and frozen treats.

Each Sunday I received a recording of sacrament meeting, helping me to feel included and valued as a member of my ward family. And every Sabbath afternoon, humble young men knelt near my bedside and sweetly, quietly administered to me the tokens of the Lord' supper. Despite being homebound, I had the privilege of renewing my sacred covenants and receiving forgiveness. Each visit included their gratifying testimonies fashioned just for me.

A friend in another state didn't let a day go by without calling to check on me—and when I had to undergo a second surgery for complications, the calls continued. Every day, there were words of solace and support from sources I never would have imagined, including a friend I hadn't seen since college. Friends and neighbors took me to doctor appointments because I could not drive myself.

---

164 Jeffrey R. Holland, *Created for Greater Things* (Salt Lake City: Deseret Book, 2011).
165 Jeffrey R. Holland, "The Ministry of Angels," *Ensign*, Nov. 2008.

What I came to learn through it all was that spiritual sustenance—the real, heartfelt, nourishing gifts that originate from our Father and Savior—make of us those angels we are meant to be. And while some may indeed include a casserole, so many are so much simpler and more meaningful.

I have learned so much . . . and likely still have much to learn. The infected wounds on my leg that drove me back into surgery will take many more weeks to heal, and I am eagerly seeking those good gifts that are in the experience for me.

Possibly more than any other thing, I have learned with a starkly new realization that our Lord and Savior Jesus Christ needs help in His mission to save a weary world from sin and sickness and despair. He needs hearts and hands that will lift and inspire and comfort those who find themselves broken and cast aside on life's long path—not only those who, like me, are suffering from physical sickness, but those who are also suffering from spiritual distress and emotional pain.

The hearts and hands He needs in that grand undertaking are yours, and they are mine.

In His mission of salvation, He needs you.

As I think about the angels who have served me and are still winging toward me with love and dedication, I know that as a woman born in this, the great winding-up scene of the earth, you have been given a special dispensation to be such an angel. Sister Camilla Eyring Kimball put it this way: "How special it is for Latter-day Saint women to be given the lofty assignments they have been given by our Father in Heaven, especially those of you who have been privileged to be born in this part of this last dispensation. . . . You can be a much-needed force for love and truth and righteousness on this planet. Let others selfishly pursue false values, but God has given to you the tremendous tasks of nurturing families, friends, and neighbors."[166]

Elder Neal A. Maxwell gave unique perspective to our charge when he wrote, "We, more than others, should carry jumper and tow cables not only in our cars, but also in our hearts, by which means we can send the needed boost or charge of encouragement or the added momentum to mortal neighbors."[167]

You may not feel that you have anything special to offer; you may worry that it is only others who have the strength or the wisdom or the creativity or the compassion to make a difference in the life of someone else. Nothing

166 Camilla Kimball, "The Role of Righteous Women," Women's Fireside, Sept. 15, 1979.
167 Neal A. Maxwell, *All These Things Shall Give Thee Experience* (Salt Lake City: Deseret Book, 2007).

could be further from the truth. You might be astonished at how simple an act can fuel the momentum of which Elder Maxwell speaks—an unassuming smile, a word of understanding, an arm slipped around sagging shoulders. As Elder David A. Bednar counseled, "Ordinary people who faithfully, diligently, and consistently do simple things that are right before God will bring extraordinary results."[168]

As a woman, you are particularly equipped by your Creator with the things needed to act as His hands and heart to His children. You can be one of those spoken of by President Russell M. Nelson when he described women "devoted to shepherding God's children along the covenant path toward exaltation"—women who know how to receive personal revelation, who teach fearlessly, and who "know how to call upon the powers of heaven to protect and strengthen children and families." He was speaking of you when he said, "You sisters possess distinctive capabilities and special intuition you have received as gifts from God. We brethren cannot duplicate your unique influence."[169]

We recognize and respect the distinctive gifts men provide as priesthood holders and as representatives of the Savior among mankind. But we as women need to equally value and celebrate our own matchless place in the Father's plan for all His children. As Elder Matthew Cowley taught, women "are born with an inherent right, an inherent authority, to be the saviors of human souls . . . and the regenerating force in the lives of God's children."[170]

If you are having trouble believing that because you are hurting or weighed down with doubt and insecurity, take courage in the words of Sister Sheri Dew, who affirmed that "Our Father has entrusted us as women with His children, and He has asked us to love them and help lead them safely past the dangers of mortality back home." In imagining those heavenly councils, she confirmed that a woman's "influence comes from a divine endowment that has been in place from the beginning in the premortal world, when our Father described our role. . . . I wonder if we shouted for joy at least in part because of the ennobling stature He gave us in His kingdom. *The world won't tell you that, but the Spirit will.*"[171]

In other words, no matter how inadequate or small or damaged you are feeling, you can lean on the Spirit and be assured that your contribution—

---

168 David A. Bednar, "Elder Bednar Teaches Women the Spiritual Pattern of Small and Simple Things," *Church News*, May 4, 2011.
169 Russell M. Nelson, "A Plea to My Sisters," *Ensign*, Nov. 2015.
170 Matthew Cowley, *Matthew Cowley Speaks* (Salt Lake City: Deseret Book, 1954), 109.
171 Sheri Dew, "Are We Not All Mothers?" *Ensign*, Nov. 2001.

whatever it is—can make an eternal difference. Your part matters because you matter. The Father and His Son stand eager to offer you any help you need in being their hands . . . as do legions of angels from beyond the veil. In organizing the Relief Society, the Prophet Joseph Smith assured women, "If you live up to your privileges, the angels cannot be restrained from being your associates."172 That promise applies today just as it did then, and you will find yourself surrounded as you work to lift and cheer and provide sustenance to those who are suffering.

Former General Relief Society President Julie B. Beck explained that our effort to provide relief to others is "the greatest, fastest solution to loneliness and hopelessness and a sure way to obtain the companionship of the Spirit. All we need to do to start offering relief is get on our knees and ask, 'Who needs my help?' Every sister—married or single, young or old—is needed in this relief effort, and it is what we should do better than anyone else."173

In seeking to take God's love to others, your effort will not look exactly like mine or like that of any other woman, but it will be of inestimable value to the soul who receives your service—your unique contribution, born of the burdens and challenges that have driven you to your knees for help and understanding.

In this, as in all other aspects of mortality, we can take for our guide the Savior of all mankind. He set the pattern for us, teaching that "whosoever will save his life shall lose it: but whosoever will lose his life for my sake, the same shall save it" (Luke 9:24).

In reflecting on the Savior's words, President Thomas S. Monson said, "I believe the Savior is telling us that unless we lose ourselves in service to others, there is little purpose to our own lives. Those who live only for themselves eventually shrivel up and . . . lose their lives, while those who lose themselves in service to others grow and flourish—and in effect save their lives."174

The Savior taught us to love, but then lived what He taught. He "went about doing good" (Acts 10:38) and "entreated all to follow his example."175 Just hours before He entered the Garden to change the outcome of all of

172 *History of the Church* 4:604–605, from a discourse given by Joseph Smith on April 28, 1842, in Nauvoo, Illinois, as reported by Eliza R. Snow.
173 Julie B. Beck, "What Latter-day Saint Women Do Best: Stand Strong and Immovable," *Ensign*, Nov. 2007.
174 Thomas S. Monson, "What Have I Done for Someone Today?" *Ensign*, Nov. 2009, 85.
175 "The Living Christ: The Testimony of the Apostles," *Ensign*, April 2000, 2.

history, He charged His disciples to "Love one another; as I have loved you" (John 13:34). And then He performed His magnificent Atonement, a sacrifice Elder Holland described as "the most majestic manifestation of pure love ever to be demonstrated in the history of this world."[176]

As we go throughout mortality, President Monson taught, we are "surrounded by those in need of our attention, our encouragement, our support, our comfort, our kindness—be they family members, friends, acquaintances, or strangers. We are the Lord's hands here upon the earth, with the mandate to serve and to lift His children. He is dependent upon each of us."[177]

He is depending on you and on me to rescue, to save. Sometimes it may require only a smile or a word of encouragement; a single rose cut from a garden; a hand-written card that arrives on a particularly discouraging day. Sometimes it may require much more. But we know that even at those times when it requires more than we ever thought we could offer, angels will be at our side and magnify our offering. It will be enough and more.

Wherever you are, whoever you are, you will never lack for those who need you. You will never be more than an arm's length from someone whose life will change because of your willingness to act as God's hands. Latter-day Saint songwriter Michael McLean referred to these souls as "refugees among us that are not from foreign shores; and the battles they are waging are from very private wars."[178] They don't carry banners or signs, he says— but are those who stand next to us in checkout lines. The story of their need for love, he writes, "is written in their eyes."

In offering that love—in being an instrument in God's hands to minister to His children, which McLean describes as a "call to arms"—you have the unparalleled opportunity to "lead anguished souls to safe harbors of the heart."

Of all the prayers that enter our hearts and cross our lips, those of greatest importance, says President Dieter F. Uchtdorf, may be the ones we answer. "Let us open our eyes and see the heavy hearts, notice the loneliness and despair; let us feel the silent prayers of those around us; and let us be an instrument in the hands of the Lord to answer those prayers."[179]

As you work to take God's love to others, a remarkable thing will happen. As in so many other instances, you will receive an astonishing measure of all

176 Jeffrey R. Holland, "Where Justice, Love, and Mercy Meet," *Ensign*, May 2014, 106.
177 Thomas S. Monson, "What Have I Done for Someone Today?" *Ensign*, 2009, 86.
178 Michael McLean, "Safe Harbors."
179 Dieter F. Uchtdorf, *The Remarkable Soul of a Woman* (Salt Lake City: Deseret Book, 2010).

you mete out, something that will bless your life as much as it blesses the lives of those you touch. For when you leave this life, writes President Henry B. Eyring, "you will feel some of the warmth and the happiness that will finally be yours when you are welcomed home again with the hundreds and perhaps thousands of others whom you will bring with you, who have walked in the light because you did."[180]

---

180 Henry B. Eyring, *Choose Higher Ground* (Salt Lake City: Deseret Book, 2013).

ABOUT THE AUTHOR

KATHRYN JENKINS GORDON IS THE managing editor at Covenant Communications, Inc. She has more than forty years of professional experience in corporate and internal communications, public relations, media relations, marketing communications, and publications management. She has been press secretary for a U.S. congressman; vice president of a Salt Lake City publishing company; manager of strategic communications for Novell, Inc.; director of public relations at a private college in Salt Lake City; and has held communications management positions at a variety of national and international corporations.

She is the author or coauthor of more than a hundred published books and wrote an award-winning book-length poetry manuscript recognized by the governor of Utah. A former member of Sigma Delta Chi, she was named an Outstanding Young Woman of America.

Her interests include reading, writing, cooking, traveling, and doing family history. She has met five presidents of the United States, sailed up the Nile River, prayed in the Garden of Gethsemane, eaten tempura in Tokyo, and received a dozen long-stemmed red roses from a stranger on the street in Athens.

She and her husband, Glenn, parent a combined and scattered family—the United States, Berlin, and Australia—of ten children and six grandchildren. And they, more than anything, are her joy in life.